Fjord pony

Haflinger

Connemara pony

Camargues pony

Welsh Mountain pony

LEARNING TO RIDE

Illustrations by Joan Thompson

AND PONY CARE all in colour

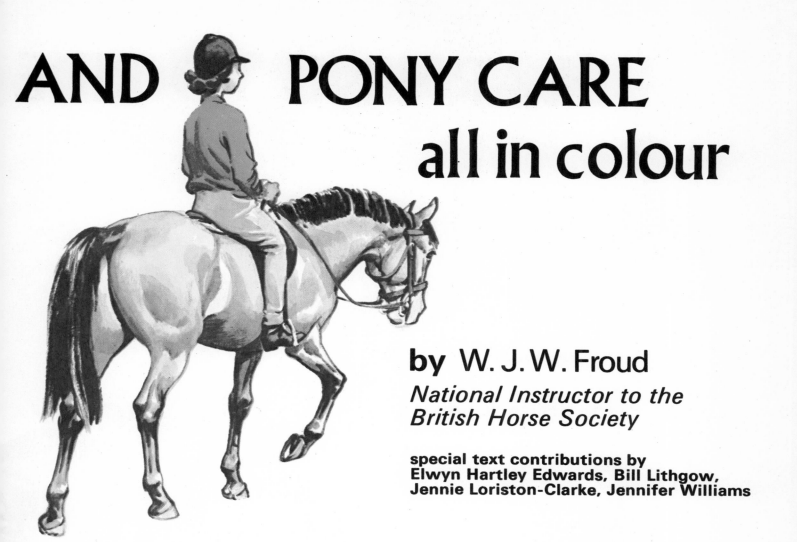

by **W. J. W. Froud**

National Instructor to the British Horse Society

**special text contributions by
Elwyn Hartley Edwards, Bill Lithgow,
Jennie Loriston-Clarke, Jennifer Williams**

First published in 1972
Second impression 1973
Third impression 1974
Fourth impression 1974
Published by William Collins Sons and Co Ltd
Glasgow and London
Copyright © 1972 Mercury Books Limited
All rights reserved
ISBN 0 00 103304 2
Printed in Tenerife (Spain) by Litografia
A. Romero, S.A. D. L. TF. 1124 - 1974

CONTENTS

Collins · Glasgow and London

UNDERSTANDING YOUR PONY

To get the best out of any horse or pony the rider must first understand a little about his instincts.

Nature's protection for the wild pony was to make him suspicious of anything he did not understand. He sought safety by running away from anything that caused him fear or pain. Even as a domesticated animal he still has this instinct, and in training him we make use of it. Knowing that he will move away from anything that causes him discomfort, we can instil in him by means of the reins and bit the habit of obedience that is essential in every well-trained pony.

The pony is not a very intelligent animal but he has an excellent memory, and this can be used to the rider's advantage when training him. *Correct* routines have to be used right from the start both in the stable and when riding because he will learn bad habits just as quickly as good ones.

One of the first things that every rider learns is that ponies are very fond of each other's company. They dislike being separated and often show great reluctance to leave the stable or paddock. A pony that gallops off into the farthest corner of the paddock every time you approach is discouraging but the rider must be patient until, after a time, obedience is gained under all circumstances.

CUPBOARD LOVERS
Ponies have one great weakness: they are all great 'cupboard lovers', fond of titbits and being fussed over. The understanding rider will encourage his pony whenever he does something that is asked of

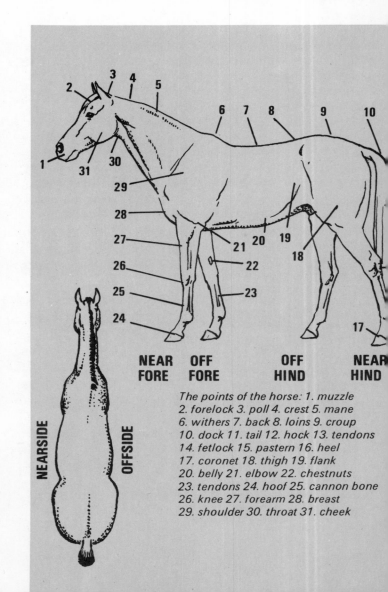

NEAR FORE   OFF FORE   OFF HIND   NEAR HIND

NEARSIDE   OFFSIDE

The points of the horse: 1. muzzle
2. forelock 3. poll 4. crest 5. mane
6. withers 7. back 8. loins 9. croup
10. dock 11. tail 12. hock 13. tendons
14. fetlock 15. pastern 16. heel
17. coronet 18. thigh 19. flank
20. belly 21. elbow 22. chestnuts
23. tendons 24. hoof 25. cannon bone
26. knee 27. forearm 28. breast
29. shoulder 30. throat 31. cheek

him by offering a tasty morsel or a friendly pat. But beware of making a fuss of him or giving him a titbit on all occasions. This will make him vicious and likely to bite if the expected offering is not forthcoming. Make sure that he understands that both titbits and fuss are *rewards* for something he has done well or tried to do.

If your pony seems nervous or reacts unexpectedly, remember that his sight and hearing are much more acute than yours. A sudden sound or movement, or a glimpse of a piece of paper fluttering nearby may be all that is needed to upset him, even ready to shy.

Watch your pony's ears. They work in close partnership with his eyes and give a very good indication of the way he is thinking. Ears pricked sharply mean that he is on the alert, not quite sure what to do. Ears laid well back are his unmistakable way of warning you that your approach or handling is unwelcome and likely to provoke a kick or a nip if it continues.

WINNING YOUR PONY'S CONFIDENCE

Knowing something about your pony's instincts, you will now see that the rider must first gain his confidence before beginning to expect obedience from him. Because horses and ponies are creatures of *habit* they will be less likely to resist if they know what to expect next. This means that the rider must do the same things in the same way at every ride.

APPROACHING YOUR PONY

In the early stages always approach from the near side, use your voice and place a reassuring hand on his neck. As long as you speak quietly and unexcitedly your voice has a calming effect. So talk gently as you approach and while you handle him. In time he will learn to associate certain words and commands with your actions. For instance, when you pick up his feet, make a point of saying 'Up' as you do so. He will soon learn to obey.

Obedience in the small things establishes the confidence between the pony and rider that makes it possible to gain obedience in the later, more advanced stages of training. The pony therefore has to learn to stand still while being groomed, saddled and rugged; he must also learn to move over when told to do so. The rider must at all times be firm but quiet, patient and encouraging. Anger or impatience will only make your pony so nervous that he will be unable to do what you want.

HANDLING

Always stand close to your pony when handling; this is the safest place, and from it you have greater control over him. Make sure that he expects your movements and is never startled by them. Sudden or unexpected handling may be enough to make him react with a kick or a nip. So learn, for example, to pick up his forelegs and hindlegs correctly.

Lifting a foreleg. Face the tail and gently slide the hand nearest the pony down his shoulder to the back of the leg. Squeeze the back tendons gently and, when your hand reaches the fetlock, say 'Up' With a young pony you may have to push your weight against his shoulder before he will lift the leg.

The correct way to lead in hand: walk alongside the pony's shoulder, reins over the head and held fairly close to the bit with the right hand, separated by the index finger. The ends of the reins are held in the left hand.

Lifting a hind leg. Again, stand close in, facing the tail, and run the hand nearest the pony down to the hock, and then inside the cannon bone. Again squeeze the back tendons slightly and give the order 'Up' as you are about to lift. Allow the lifted leg to go naturally to the rear but do not try to lift it high (*see the illustrations on page 47*).

LEADING IN HAND

Most ponies that have been handled as foals will follow if led quietly by rope or reins. Again, stand on the near side and always take the reins over the pony's head before moving forward. The correct way is shown in the illustration, with the ends of the reins in the left hand, and the right hand holding both reins fairly close to the bit, separated by the index finger.

Stand by the pony's shoulder, give the command 'Walk on' and then quietly walk forward alongside. Do not pull!

When leading a pony through a stable door, look back to make sure that he is clear of the doorposts. Careless leading can cause him to knock his hip as he comes through.

WHAT TO WEAR

If you are proud of your pony, your dress and his turnout should always do you both credit. Riding clothes should be neat, clean and workmanlike. Because they are fairly expensive they are usually made of good material and the probability is that they will last well and have a lot of wear left in them long after their first owner has outgrown them. So handing down from an elder brother or sister or friend makes good sense. The fact that the clothes are not brand new does not matter provided that they fit and are comfortable.

For hacking and daily work you should wear:

> *hard hat*
> *windcheater (subdued colour)*
> *roll-necked pullover*
> *jodhpurs*
> *jodhpur boots, rubber riding boots or*
> *   strong leather shoes*

For showing or hunting both rider and pony should be as smart as possible: you should wear:

> *hard hat*
> *riding jacket*
> *white shirt and tie*
> *jodhpur breeches*
> *jodhpur boots*

For informal rides (hacking and daily work) a roll-necked sweater and windcheater are practical and comfortable.

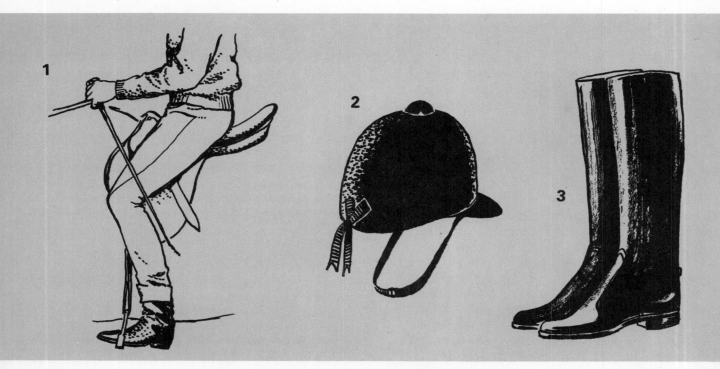

For more formal occasions (shows and hunting) a dark riding jacket, white shirt and tie are more suitable.

HATS

For safety and comfort you should always wear a well-fitting hard hat (with a chin strap if you are jumping). Dark blue or black velvet riding hats are the most popular. Whatever the hat you choose, buy it from a reputable firm specialising in riding clothes or hats.

The hat should be worn well down on your forehead with hair tucked tidily underneath and none showing under the peak of the hat.

RIDING JACKETS

These are of a special cut so that they fit neatly and comfortably when you are mounted. They may be of any colour but soft tweedy mixtures in subdued tones are considered the most suitable. Until you are older you do not really need a black riding jacket.

JODHPURS

These are so well made nowadays that finding a pair of stretch jodhpurs to give a good smart fit is an easy matter. For warmth and to save being rubbed nylon tights underneath are excellent for girl riders.

BOOTS AND SHOES

Elastic-sided boots are neat, comfortable and correct. Shoes may be worn but they must be made of leather and must have a heel to stop your foot slipping through the stirrup iron.

Rubber riding boots are wonderful labour savers and can be worn on most occasions provided they fit well and are kept clean.

RIDING MAC AND GLOVES

A good raincoat is necessary for wet weather rides. If you are hacking across some distance it can be tied across the front of the saddle, fastened to the D's which are on most saddles.

Gloves should be worn on formal occasions and when it is wet. String ones are the most suitable because they do not slip and are reasonably warm.

Clothes care is almost as important as care of saddlery. Boots should be cleaned and other items hung up neatly after use.

1. How to hold a schooling whip: in your left hand and lying obliquely across your thigh. When needed use it lightly behind the girth—and without taking your hand from the reins.

2. A well-fitting reinforced riding cap is the rider's most important item of equipment. Wear it—always—with the peak well down over your forehead for protection.

3. Rubber riding boots are less trouble to keep clean than leather topboots—and much less expensive.

4. In wet weather a riding mac with leg straps to hold it in place across your thighs, and a vent at the back to allow it to fall across the saddle, will keep you dry. String gloves will help you to keep a firm grip on the reins.

MOUNTING AND DISMOUNTING

The pony must stand still and squarely on all four legs while the rider mounts. Clumsy, rough movements will upset and confuse him, so the rider's actions must be neat, deliberate and quiet.

CHECKS BEFORE MOUNTING
The reins should be taken over the pony's head and lie evenly on the neck. Check that the girth is tight and the stirrup irons down. A rough guide for the stirrup length is the length of the rider's own arm; place the stirrup under your armpit, then adjust the leather so that your knuckles reach the stirrup buckle.

MOUNTING
Stand level with the pony's nearside shoulder, facing the rear; with the left hand take the reins and grasp the pony's mane or wither. With the right hand hold the stirrup leather and put your left foot well into the iron with the toe pointing downwards. Grasp the back of the saddle with your right hand. Then spring up from your right foot, straighten your left knee and swing your right leg over the saddle, pivoting yourself over and clear of the pony's back. At the same time transfer your right hand to the arch of the saddle. Lower yourself *gently* into the saddle. Finally, take your right stirrup, and a rein in each hand.

Your pony must stand still when being mounted and for at least five seconds once you are in the saddle.

DISMOUNTING
Take both feet out of the stirrups. Place both hands on the front of the saddle, lean the body forward and vault off on the nearside of the pony, making sure that your right leg is well clear of his back. The reins remain one in each hand as you do so. Land lightly on your toes and facing forwards.

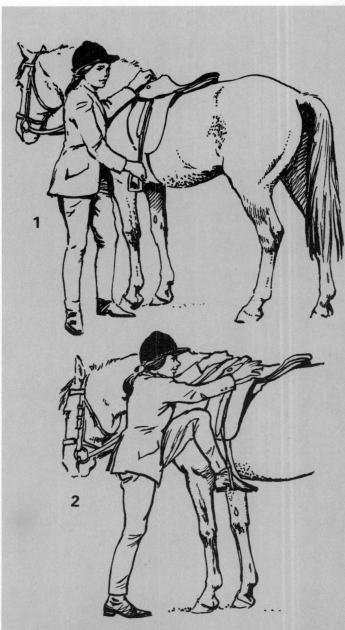

At the halt make sure you are sitting centrally in the saddle with your back straight, eyes front and reins just gently taut but not strained. Ideally there should be a straight line from the bit through your wrist to your elbow.

Mounting: the actual mounting procedure is described on the opposite page. At Stage 1 your pony should be standing quite still before you attempt to mount. At Stage 2 be careful not to jab your pony's sides with your toe. At Stage 3 swing your leg well clear of his back and settle into the saddle gently. Wait until he has adjusted his balance to your weight before moving off.

Dismounting: the method of dismounting is described opposite. Keep hold of the reins so that you remain in control, and steady yourself with your hand on the arch of the saddle if necessary.

11

A central-position saddle will help you achieve the 'in balance' position.

DEVELOPING A GOOD SEAT

All good riding is based on a firm, well balanced seat. It takes time to develop the firm seat but from the very beginning every rider can and must learn to sit 'in balance'. Unless you work to get this position right you will never be in complete harmony with your pony and you will not develop the sensitive hands that every good horseman has.

IN BALANCE
The 'in-balance' position is at the lowest part of the pony's back, immediately behind the withers. A good central-position saddle is essential to help you to sit in the right place without effort. It will also help keep your weight off the pony's loins.

To be correctly 'in balance' there should be a straight line through the rider's shoulders, down through his hips to his heels — even if at first this means that the knees have to come away from the saddle a little.

BODY AND HEAD
Your body must be upright but supple, ready to conform to the pony's movements at all paces. Your head should be held straight and high, with eyes looking front.

LEGS
Correctly adjusted stirrup leathers play a part in achieving the 'in balance' position. They should be adjusted to a length that is comfortable and gives you support. If they are too short your knee will be cramped and you will be pushed to the rear. If they are too long you will be tipped forward.

With the leathers correctly adjusted the thighs will lie softly against the saddle without pressure. The knees must not be pinched in against the saddle flap, but relaxed to allow the lower leg to fall back naturally against the pony's sides.

FEET
Your ankles act as springs, cushioning you against the action of the ride, and must not be locked stiffly. Your heel should be a little lower than the toe, which should lie at a natural angle, with the inside of your boot against the pony's side. Only the ball of your foot (its broadest part) rests on the stirrup iron.

HANDS AND ARMS
Your arms should be held in a natural position so that the elbows can be soft, your fingers and wrists supple. Your upper arm should hang naturally from the

Above: the correct 'in balance' position is immediately behind the withers. Shoulders, hips and heels should be in a straight line.

Below: the leathers of correctly adjusted stirrups should hang vertically, just long enough to give support to your foot.

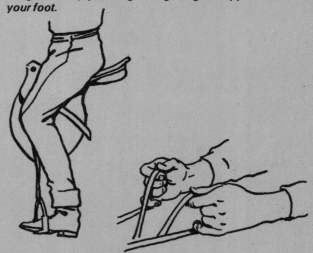

The correct way to hold the reins of a snaffle bridle

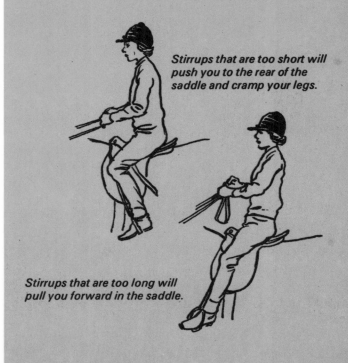

Stirrups that are too short will push you to the rear of the saddle and cramp your legs.

Stirrups that are too long will pull you forward in the saddle.

shoulder, and when the rein is taut (but not strained) your elbow should be just forward of your hip. Elbows should never be allowed to go behind the hips; this means the reins are too long and stiffen your body.

A good position gives a straight line through the elbow, along the forearm to the bit.

HOLDING THE REINS

The reins of a snaffle bridle should be held one in each hand, passing below the fourth finger through the palm of the hand, and held by the thumb and first finger. The hands must always be held level, one on each side of the pony's neck, just over the pommel, with knuckles to the front, thumbs uppermost and wrists flexible.

The pony should now be led round at a walk while you try to keep a *light* contact with his mouth as his head swings up and down. The reins should feel just 'stretched', like a piece of elastic. As long as the pony is moving in the direction and at the pace you want, simply let your hands follow the movement with this light, elastic contact. Light hands are the hallmark of a good rider. Heavy hands will make a mouth insensitive.

Allow your hips to swing with the movement too, so that you can begin to feel and get the rhythm of the ride in hands and body.

HOW TO IMPROVE YOUR BALANCE

1. For the arms: at the halt and without stirrups, swing your arms one at a time, windmill fashion, six times forwards and six times backwards. Keep the movement under control and the rest of your body as still as possible.

Riding is a very active exercise and uses muscles which are not often made to work. If you are to enjoy your riding they must be developed gradually over a period of time.

Your natural balance must also be developed to ensure that you can follow the pony's movements smoothly.

To maintain your seat in the saddle you must develop these muscles correctly so that they can be controlled instantly, and allow you to apply precisely and confidently the aids by which you will learn to control the pony. These aids are described on page 18.

The more you stretch your muscles the more supple you will become, and the more supple you are the greater your control over the pony will be. Working at the halt and without stirrups is excellent for this, provided you keep your thigh and lower leg in the correct position. But too much work without stirrups or trotting too soon without them will make your muscles tired, and tired muscles soon force the rider to adopt an incorrect position to ease them. This encourages the very faults the exercises are intended to improve. Muscles, like ponies, have to be brought into peak condition gradually.

Practise these simple exercises for a few minutes at the beginning of every ride and you will soon have a seat that is firm and in balance, with each part of your body capable of acting effortlessly and independently.

First, *at the halt and without stirrups*, reins on your pony's neck, practise exercises 1, 2 and 3

As a last exercise, take your stirrups and your reins at the correct length. Now, *still at the halt*, with head straight and eyes looking forward, raise your seat about three inches from the saddle without increasing the tension on the reins. Stay standing in your stirrups for a few seconds and then gently lower your seat back into the saddle. If you cannot perform this exercise standing still, you are not sitting in balance.

14

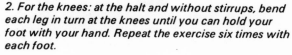

2. *For the knees: at the halt and without stirrups, bend each leg in turn at the knees until you can hold your foot with your hand. Repeat the exercise six times with each foot.*

4. *For hip and back muscles: at the halt but this time with your feet in the stirrups, hold the pommel with two fingers of each hand. Lift both thighs three inches or so out of the saddle, keeping your knees bent and your back straight. You should be able to feel the weight of your body on your seat bones. Relax and then repeat six times.*

3. *For back and neck muscles: at the halt and without stirrups stretch your knees down and back to the rear of the saddle flap. At the same time stretch your head and spine upwards and look into the sky. Relax the muscles. Repeat six times. This exercise will supple your back and also encourage you to keep your head straight.*

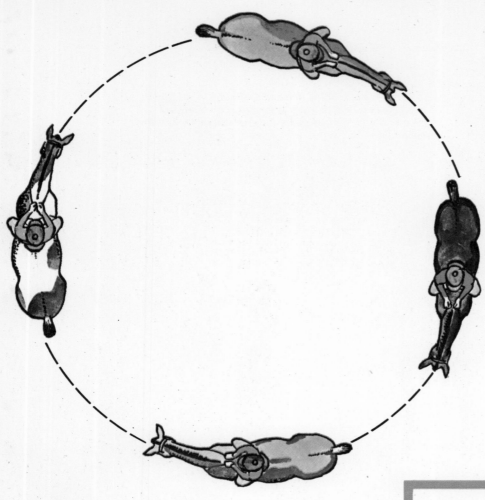

FIRST LESSONS

Above: accurate circling between markers in the manege teaches you to use the aids correctly and keeps the pony supple. The pony must bend along the line of the movement with his hind feet following in the tracks of his fore-feet. When you circle to the left you are 'riding on the left rein', and when you circle to the right you are 'riding on the right rein'.

Right: incorrect circling. The pony's hindquarters have swung outwards from the line of movement and his hind feet no longer follow in the tracks of his forefeet.

Below: four basic school movements. 1. forming a double ride. 2. crossing the school 3. serpentining 4. inclining across the school. When executed between markers these exercises teach you precision and the correct use of the aids.

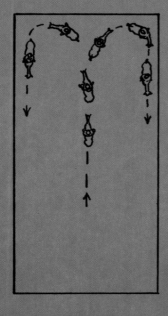
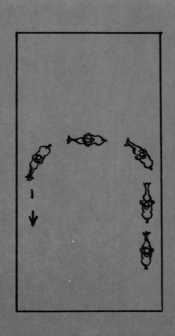
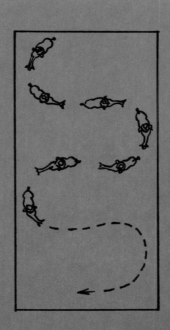
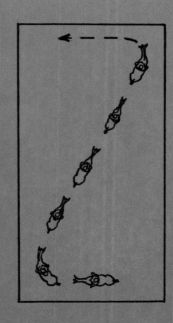

It is a great help to both a young pony and a young rider if the first lessons can be taken in an enclosed space. This gives you confidence and enables you to concentrate on what is required without being distracted.

THE MANEGE

Ideally an indoor riding school is the best place to begin, but a manege in a quiet corner of a field, provided it is enclosed by a fence or bales of straw can be quite adequate.

The manege should be of the correct dimensions and with correct markers, as shown in the illustration. The markers teach you to ride accurately: once you can ride on a straight line from one marker to another and ride a true circle between them, it means that your pony is becoming responsive and obedient and that you are applying your aids correctly. If your pony learns to obey you in the manege, it will of course be easier to obtain obedience from him when riding in the open country.

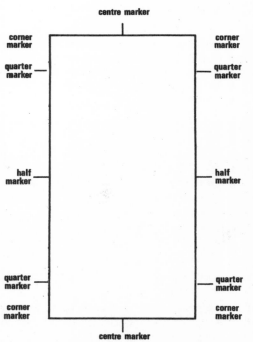

A manege with centre, halfway and quarter markers. The correct dimensions are 44 yards long by 22 yards wide.

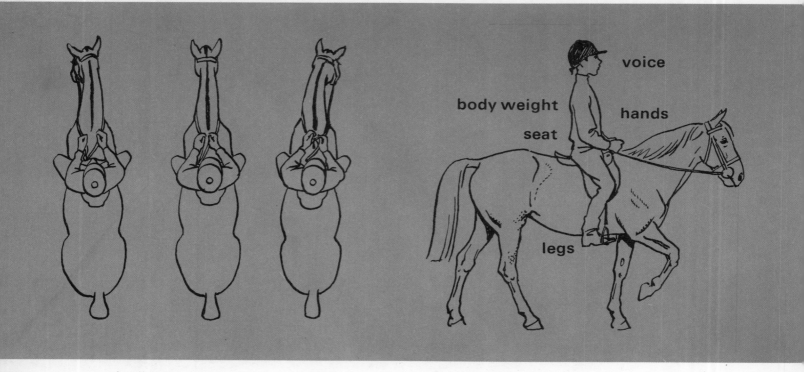

body weight

voice

hands

seat

legs

THE RIDER'S NATURAL AIDS

The rider conveys his wishes to the trained pony by a number of signals called *aids*. These tell the pony that his rider wants to change pace or direction, to move forward, halt and so on. To use the aids effectively the rider must know how and when to apply them, and the pony must be trained to understand and obey them.

Unless you apply the aids correctly the pony will not respond and will become confused. To ride well therefore you must study the effects on your pony and then practise them until he obeys easily and willingly.

The novice rider can only learn the true effect of the aids by riding a *trained* pony who already knows what each aid signals. Trying to master them on an untrained pony will be a depressing experience because the pony will not understand what is wanted of him and the rider will be likely to resort to force, which should never be necessary in a well-teamed combination of horse and rider.

The voice. This is the aid which links obedience on the ground and the beginning of obedience on your pony's back. You have already learned how to make him 'walk on' and 'halt' when you are dismounted (page 7). Now, when mounted, you squeeze gently at the girth with your legs and give the command 'Walk on' — words he already understands and will respond to. Very quickly he will obey this leg pressure without the spoken command.

Similarly he will obey a slight resistance with the reins and the command 'whoa' or 'halt'. But make sure that your voice is never loud or aggressive — and never use it in the show ring, where it will incur faults.

Weight. The weight of your body through your seat is a very effective aid when used correctly. The problem for a beginner is, in the first instance, to keep the weight central. When you can do this without effort then you are ready to use your weight as an aid.

Legs. The first function of your legs is to produce and maintain forward movement. This leads to impulsion, the basis of all training. Their second function is to control the pony's hindquarters. They give the aid either at the girth or immediately behind it, depending on the movement you require.

Light pressure applied at the girth by the legs urges the pony forward. They should be kept still and close to the pony's sides ready for instant use. But take care not to flap them continuously. This will only serve to deaden your pony's sensitive sides and make him unresponsive to this aid.

Your pony is showing greater obedience and more suppleness in the hindquarters when he responds to light pressure from one leg only used *behind* the girth, moving his quarters sideways to the right when the left leg exerts the pressure, and to the left when the right leg exerts it.

The hands. Your hands are all important: through the reins and bit they guide and control the impulsion created by your legs. They also control the pony's forehand — just as your legs control the hindquarters.

Many novice riders wrongly think that the way to get obedience is to tug hard on the reins. Nothing could be more mistaken. A good rider has soft elbows and supple wrists. These allow the hands to remain passive under most circumstances, simply following the movements of the pony's head and neck. On an increase of pace your hands should follow the movement. On a decrease of pace they should resist slightly, but should never exert a 'pull' by drawing back.

ARTIFICIAL AIDS

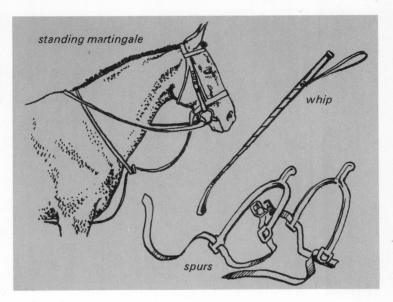

standing martingale

whip

spurs

running martingale

THE WHIP

A flexible whip about 3 feet long should be carried when schooling a pony. A smooth, slender ash plant cut from the hedge is ideal. This can be used to reinforce the rider's leg aids *with a light tap* behind the girth when the pony's response is not quick enough. It should be held in the left hand, lying obliquely across the rider's thigh and pointing towards the ground (see diagram page 8). *It should be used without removing* the hand from the rein.

It is much better to use a schooling whip than to overwork the leg aids, as excessive use of the legs will render your pony callous to them.

To use the shorter whip carried when jumping you will have to remove your hand from the rein. It should be used *behind the girth* only when a definite disobedience has taken place.

SPURS

Spurs are for applying more refined aids and should be worn only by a highly skilled rider on a well-trained horse. A young horse should be trained initially without spurs.

MARTINGALES

There are two kinds of martingale: *running* and *standing.* Their purpose is to lower the pony's head so that he can be more easily controlled and will round his back when jumping.

Ideally, all horses and ponies should be schooled to go properly without any form of martingale or auxiliary to the bit.

The running martingale is useful so long as it is properly fitted so that when the pony's head is held in the right place the rings of the martingale do not affect the rein action. The martingale then comes into play only if the pony tries to get his head above the angle of control.

A standing martingale holds the pony's head down forcibly and may be used if there is a danger of him throwing his head so high that he is likely to hit his rider in the face or become uncontrollable. It must be fitted so that the pony can carry his head with his muzzle level with the base of the withers.

CHANGING PACE AND DIRECTION

turning on the open rein

Turning right by the open rein method: the right hand is carried outwards and this leads the pony's nose gently round to the right. Until you have learned to use the diagonal aid you will change direction by the open rein method.

It is a common fault for riders to use their hands too much and their legs too little. Both should work in harmony. Your seat and, when necessary, your legs must always be used *before* your hands when increasing and decreasing pace.

INCREASING PACE.
On an increase of pace from halt to walk, the pony must first engage his hindquarters to propel himself forward. The correct procedure for you is:

1. *Put your weight on your seat bones*
2. *Apply both legs at the girth*
3. *Ease both reins*

The pony will then move forward.

DECREASING PACE
On a decrease of pace from walk to halt the pony must again engage his hindquarters because they are his braking power as well as his accelerating power. The correct procedure for you is:

1. *Put your weight on your seat bones*
2. *Apply both legs at the girth*
3. *Resist lightly through the reins*

The pony will then decrease pace on a straight line, with a steady head carriage and no resistance. If there is any sign of resistance through the mouth or any

With the inside leg (i.e. the left) ask the pony to go forward and encourage him to bend by applying the leg aid.

With the outside leg (i.e. the right) a little behind the girth ask for impulsion and control any swing of the hind quarters so that the hind feet follow in the tracks of the forefeet.

Resist with the left hand to give direction.

'Allow' with the right hand by 'giving' a little but keeping control of the pace.

the diagonal aid : turning to the left

swing in his hindquarters you will know that you have been guilty of using tactless hands.

At the halt the pony should be taught to stand squarely on all four legs.

TURNING: THE OPEN REIN METHOD

It is fairly obvious that when you want to change course your pony must look in the direction you want him to follow. By the constant use of the correct aids he will eventually become supple enough for his whole body to bend on the line of the movement. Until then he will rely largely on the turn of his head. So, in the early stages, when you wish to turn right you will use the *open rein* method:

1. Apply the leg aid to ask the pony to go forward
2. Carry your right hand outwards (this leads the pony's nose to the right so that he follows it in a soft turn)

For a left turn follow the same procedure but carry the *left* hand out to produce the bend.

THE DIAGONAL AID

As your control improves and your pony becomes more responsive you will not need to carry your hand out in order to change direction. Instead of the open rein you will be ready to apply *the diagonal aid*, in which your *inside hand* (the one on the side to which you wish to turn) will produce the bend by resisting, and your *outside hand* will 'allow' the bend by yielding.

RIGHT AND LEFT TURNS

The correct procedure for a *left* turn is given above:

The correct procedure for a right turn is the same but substituting left for right and right for left in the instructions above.

The diagonal aid is one in which each hand and each leg has a different task to perform, but all work harmoniously to produce the required turn. The emphasis you give to each hand and leg depends on the degree of the turn you want.

Great care must be taken that the aids do not work against each other: if the right hand asks for the bend, the left must allow it, and if the right leg asks for a certain movement, the left leg must be ready to yield to it but control it.

Remember: the seat and legs demand the movement; the hands guide and control it.

PRACTISING THE AIDS

Now that you know how to apply the basic aids, practise them regularly *at the walk*, working in the manege: halt to walk, walk to halt, advancing on straight lines, turns and circles. Ride to markers and concentrate on making your movements accurate.

THE PACES

1

THE WALK

The walk is a pace of *4 time*, in which the pony lifts each leg separately in this sequence: *1. near hind 2. near fore 3. off hind 4. off fore*.

The walk should be long striding, with the pony allowed to use his head and neck. It must be energetic but calm. It is an excellent pace for steady exercise, because each leg does the same amount of work with little strain on the feet and limbs.

The walk is an excellent pace for steady exercise, giving each leg the same amount of work. The pony's feet are lifted in this order: 1. near hind. 2. near fore. 3. off hind. 4. off fore.

THE TROT

The trot is a pace of *2 time,* with the pony's feet coming down in alternate diagonal pairs: *1. near fore and off hind together* (the left diagonal) *and 2. off fore* and *near hind* together (the right diagonal).

In an active trot there is a moment of suspension when all four feet are off the ground together.

The trot is a good schooling pace because it is an even pace with natural impulsion and the pony's head is comparatively still.

The pony on the left is on the left diagonal (near fore and off hind on the ground). The pony on the right is on the right diagonal (off fore and near hind on the ground).

Both the canter and the gallop have a moment of suspension when the pony has all four legs off the ground.

THE CANTER

The canter is a pace of *3 time.* It is active, exhilarating and much more tiring than the trot. The pony must be kept calm.

To enable a pony to change direction safely when cantering he must canter with the *inside foreleg* and *inside hind leg* leading.

So, cantering to the left (with the near fore leading) the footfalls would be: *1. off hind 2. right diagonal (off fore and near hind) 3. near fore.*

Cantering to the right the footfalls would be: *1. near hind 2. left diagonal (near fore and off hind) 3. off fore.*

If a pony canters incorrectly, with the near fore leading on a right-hand canter or the near hind leading on a left canter, it is called *cantering false.*

Disunited canter (caused by loss of balance or bad training) occurs when the leading foreleg and the leading hind leg are on the opposite sides.

THE GALLOP

The gallop is an increased or lengthened canter whose second beat (the diagonal) is broken into two separate beats as the pony stretches into the gallop.

To avoid excitement and pulling a pony must be trained to gallop very gradually. Both the canter and the gallop have a moment of suspension with all four legs off the ground at the end of each stride.

THE RIDER AT WALK AND TROT

AT THE WALK

The position for the walk is the same as at the halt (page 11) except that your body conforms to the pony's movement and your hand keeps a light contact. In fact, you maintain this basic position at *all* paces with certain modifications. Whatever the pace the rider must always look forward. This improves your balance and keeps your back and loins erect. Looking down causes rounded shoulders and slack loins, making your seat unstable and out of balance.

Sit firmly on your seat bones. If you lean forward you lose the influence of the seat and weight your hands and legs so that you cannot apply your aids effectively.

By working at the walk you will be able to concentrate on perfecting your position and on the application of the aids in preparation for the faster pace of the trot.

THE TROT

There are two ways of riding the trot: sitting and rising. Before attempting either of them you should get the *feel* of the trotting rhythm.

The trotting rhythm. Sit as for the halt, but with both reins in the left hand, lightly holding the front of the saddle with the right. Apply the leg aid and walk forward. Squeeze the pony's sides again with both legs and ease your hands on the reins. Your pony will increase his pace to a *slow trot*. Steady yourself in the saddle with your right hand. Knees and ankles should be kept supple. After a few strides decrease the pace to a walk again by applying the same aid that you used for walk-to-halt.

This will give you some idea of what the trotting rhythm feels like. Try to count the 2-time beat with your seat kept firmly in the saddle at each step.

At this point it is better to move on to the *rising trot* before attempting to master the *sitting trot*, which requires more highly developed muscles and is best left until a little later.

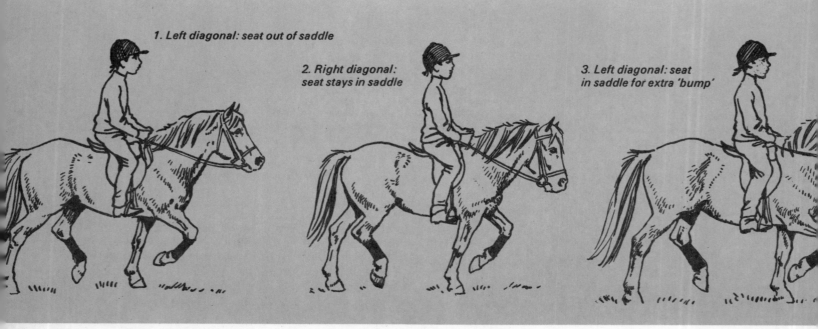

1. Left diagonal: seat out of saddle

2. Right diagonal: seat stays in saddle

3. Left diagonal: seat in saddle for extra 'bump'

the hips with the movement and let your shoulders go forward with your hips. You must look forward. And keep your elbows soft so that your hands don't bob up and down and pass the movement through the bit to the pony's mouth.

RISING TROT EXERCISES
The same exercises that were performed at the walk (page 20) should now be practised in rising trot: increase and decrease of pace (trot to walk and walk to trot), change of direction and so on. There must be a minimum use of leg and hand. Use the schooling whip lightly if the pony's response is not immediate.

All movements must be carried out with great accuracy, so ride precisely to markers, keeping the turns, circles and direction changes soft and easy. To begin with, a working circle with a diameter of 20 metres is practical and will give you and the pony a chance. As you both become more proficient you can reduce the diameter of the circle and make the exercise more difficult. But first concentrate on accuracy and smoothness while riding on the bigger circle.

THE SITTING TROT
The sitting trot is a very useful exercise but because it is extremely tiring for the muscles you should not keep it up for long periods until you can sit upright without gripping hard with knees and thigh. To begin with hold the saddle with your right hand and the reins with your left. This will stop you from slipping to the back of the saddle and help to keep your body upright. Heels should be kept under your shoulder position, as at the halt and walk. The sitting trot should not be used on a young horse or pony until his muscles are strong enough to accept the weight.

Practise for short periods, holding and letting go of the saddle until you begin to feel confident of your balance. Don't hurry the pace. Stick to a slow jog until you and the pony are quite sure of yourselves. Once you feel fully confident you can take the reins in both hands and practise the exercise without the supporting hand on the saddle.

THE RISING TROT
This is an exercise the rider must learn to perform in balance and without excessive movement. The rising-at-halt exercise on page 15 is an ideal preparation for it.

The rising trot is easier than the sitting trot for both the pony and the rider and is used in the early stages of training and also when hacking or riding over long distances.

Shoulders should be carried slightly forward, seat just rising from the saddle as one diagonal comes to the ground and falling back gently as the other diagonal comes down: up on one beat and down on the next. The lower legs should be behind the perpendicular and kept close in to the pony's sides. Knees should be supple. If they grip tightly this stiffens you and makes your seat stick out. Rise from

ht diagonal: seat out
dle (diagonal has been changed)

Changing diagonals: in the trot the pony's feet strike the ground in diagonal pairs. In rising trot the rider's seat is in contact with the saddle as one pair of diagonals hits the ground, and slightly out of the saddle when the other pair does so.

A novice rider usually rises on one diagonal and falls on the other every time. This is wrong and makes the pony stiff on one side and lacking flexibility. He should trot evenly on both diagonals, and to ensure that he does so, you must learn to change diagonals throughout the ride. In riding school it is usual to change the diagonal when you change rein, normally riding on the outside one (that is, with the seat coming down into the saddle as the outside diagonal comes to the ground).

Learning to change diagonals is simply a matter of keeping your seat in the saddle for an extra 'bump' instead of rising. The diagrams show the sequence of the rider's rise and fall in the saddle.

TROTTING POLES

A good exercise in your school or manege at this stage is to start work over poles on the ground. Correct use of trotting poles improves your balance and produces the right reflexes in pony and rider. It is an excellent preliminary to jumping. It teaches the pony to negotiate a series of poles by adjusting his balance and strides – something he will have to do over fences. He learns to respect the poles without getting excited or nervous and to stretch his head and neck and relax his back muscles.

Start him off over one pole, heavy enough not to roll if he touches it as he walks over it. Walk him quietly over, going straight both before and after, and turning correctly at each end of your walk. Repeat this once or twice until he is clearing the pole without hesitation each time.

Add a second pole about four-and-a-half feet away from the first (the actual distance will depend on the stride of your pony). Again walk him quietly over them until he is stepping clear each time.

Now increase your pace to a rising trot; your shoulders should be slightly further forward, and the rhythm of the trot kept fairly slow.

Gradually introduce extra poles one at a time until you have six. With patience your pony will learn to swing his back and use his hocks, and you will learn to sit in balance and maintain light contact as he steps over the poles.

To be a successful jumper your pony must have a calm approach, and this is one of the benefits gained by working over the poles before going on to actual jumps. It introduces him gradually to obstacles and the *idea* of getting over them.

Introduce your pony to trotting poles gradually, teaching him first to step over one, then adding poles one at a time until he is able to negotiate a line of six or so. Ride precisely, coming in straight, first at the walk and then increasing the pace to a rising trot when you are both confident.

THE CANTER

canter to the right

At this pace there is a complete change of rhythm, a faster pace and a swinging motion from the pony's head. Before attempting it you must be well prepared by plenty of work in rising and sitting trot. Work over the trotting poles will help your balance and increase the suppleness of loins, knees and ankles — essential in trying to obtain a good position at the canter.

At first hold the saddle with the *outside hand*, and the reins — fairly short — with the *inside hand*.

First teach your pony to lead off correctly by striking off out of a corner or on a circle. This will enable him to lead off correctly with the inside foreleg.

In sitting trot apply both legs, using *the inside leg at the girth* and *the outside leg behind the girth*. As your pony strikes off, your pelvis will be pulled forward by the hand holding the saddle. This helps to keep your back straight and allows your body to follow the rocking rhythm.

When the seat feels secure, let go of the saddle and take a rein in each hand, but always be ready to pull yourself forward by the saddle again if necessary.

RIDER'S POSITION
The rhythm of the canter requires your back to be stretched upright and your heels in line below your ankles to give true flexibility and balance. Rounding your back is no substitute for suppleness. In fact it does the opposite and stiffens you, thus preventing you from applying your aids correctly.

Your head must be straight and looking forward. Looking down and to one side makes you stiff and upsets your balance.

At the canter the pony's head swings, and the rider's hand must follow this perfectly natural motion — just as it did at the walk. The shoulders should appear to be still and the rider's legs are kept close to the pony's sides.

TRANSITIONS
Practise the transitions from trot to canter and from canter to trot until you have completely adjusted to the new rhythm.

Decreasing pace from canter to trot must be done in a balanced manner. The pony should not fall on his forehand and the rider should maintain his position. With the rider bracing his back slightly, seat pushed up to the front, legs close to the pony's sides and hands resisting the movement, the transition to the trot is smoothly made.

canter to the left

Try to keep your hands light and aim to develop your seat to be quite independent of the reins. Unless you do this you cannot apply the correct aids.

AIDS TO CANTER
It has already been explained (page 23) that to take a turn or circle smoothly, easily and safely a pony must canter with the correct leg leading. To do so he must also be taught the correct aids to strike off on the desired leg.

First teach him to trot on a large circle to the left. In sitting trot with your pony looking slightly into the circle, apply both legs, with the *outside leg just behind the girth*. The aid must be clear and distinct. Both legs are important: the inside leg at the girth prepares the canter while the outside leg, just behind the girth, signals the canter with a slight nudge.

When your pony understands the aid and will canter freely on both legs, you can make the exercise more difficult by striking off from the incline and eventually on the straight. When you can do this you will have achieved a high standard of obedience and can feel satisfied that you and the pony have profited permanently from learning the aids so thoroughly.

To canter correctly the pony must lead off with the inside foreleg and the inside hind leg. Practise the canter aids riding in large circles to left and right until he is striking off correctly in both directions.

Once your pony has learned to clear a line of cavaletti, as shown on page 35, you can begin work at a 'box' of cavaletti, jumping quietly from every direction and coming back to a trot after each pair of jumps. Guide, control and regulate the pace without kicking, pushing or pulling.

LEARNING TO JUMP AND CAVALETTI WORK

Any new exercise should be introduced to the pony and the rider in the easiest possible way. Jumping is no exception. The pony has to perform a more violent action by propelling himself through the air, and the rider has to learn to stay in balance while he does so and eventually control the movement.

If your work over the trotting poles has been progressively carried out, the pony should now be trotting actively but calmly down six poles while you keep in balance riding trot and maintain the lightest of contacts through the bit.

PREPARING FOR A LOW JUMP

You should now prepare for the next step: a low jump. Shorten your stirrup leathers by two holes. This will give you greater leverage of the thigh, and enable you to stay in balance more easily without altering your position greatly.

A good preliminary exercise to jumping is to trot round the manege with shoulders forward and your seat about one inch clear of the saddle without any increased tension on the reins.

This is a good balancing exercise and it also teaches you to keep the lower leg in the right place by holding the saddle with the part of the leg just below the knee, at the same time keeping the knee joint supple; this is very important.

Now, beyond a row of trotting poles set a cavaletto 18 inches high and about 8 feet from your last pole. Your trotting poles will bring the pony in quietly with you sitting in balance as before; as the pony takes off over the small jump, bend your body slightly forward to reduce the angle between it and your thighs. Very little movement is needed. Your hands follow the movement of the pony's head, going slightly forward as he tops the fence and coming back as he lands. The pony must go straight forward after the fence and be brought back to his normal rising trot.

THE RIDER'S POSITION

The first essential, as always, is for the rider to learn to sit still, just conforming to the pony's movement, and aim to perfect an 'in balance' position and follow the movement of the head and neck.

Now increase the difficulty of the exercise by adding a second cavaletto about 15 feet from the first. This distance will give the average pony one canter stride between the two jumps. Again, the rider must sit still; quietness on approach, jumping and going away is the aim. Until you achieve this with complete confidence no further progress can be made.

In the excitement of jumping many riders forget to ride correctly on the flat. This is something that must be avoided. The pony must continue to turn correctly, and increase and decrease pace smoothly, with the rider always paying attention to his position and applying his aids properly.

Markers to encourage you to ride accurately are always a great help at this stage. Five-gallon oil drums are excellent for this purpose and are easily obtained.

Gradually increase the number of cavaletti and vary the distance between them — one stride, two strides, no strides. But make certain that your distances are correct for your particular pony; if he makes mistakes at this stage he may lose his confidence. Continue to keep the fences low for the same reason.

You can now put two cavaletti together to make a spread about two feet six inches wide; this will encourage your pony to round his back as he clears them, and to use his head and neck more.

Finally in this exercise you can remove the trotting poles one by one, until your pony will trot into the first jump quietly and in a balanced manner.

Shorten your stirrup leathers by two holes for jumping. Bring your pony into a low jump at the trot and in a straight line, quietly and without rushing. As he takes off, bend your body slightly forward to reduce the angle between it and your thighs. Your hands should simply follow the movement of the pony's head, coming forward slightly as he clears the fence.

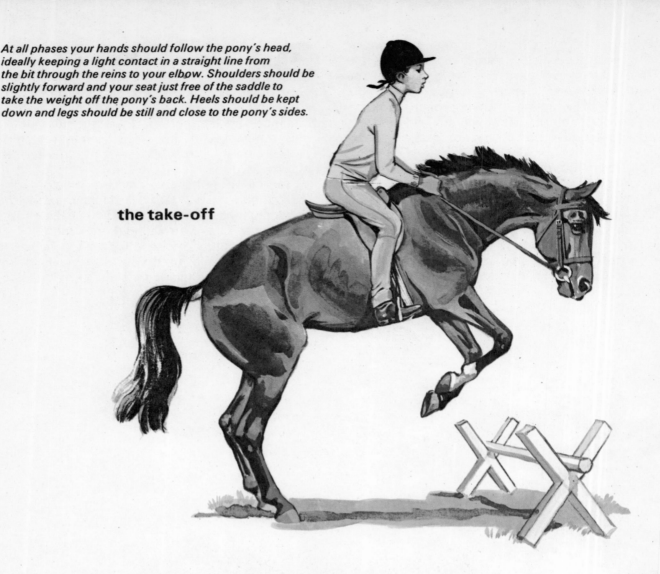

At all phases your hands should follow the pony's head, ideally keeping a light contact in a straight line from the bit through the reins to your elbow. Shoulders should be slightly forward and your seat just free of the saddle to take the weight off the pony's back. Heels should be kept down and legs should be still and close to the pony's sides.

the take-off

THE PHASES
OF THE JUMP

There are four phases to the jump: the approach, the take-off, the clearance and the landing. The most important part of the jump is the approach. This is why we teach the pony first to come in at a trot, without rushing and with a steady head carriage. This gives him a chance to jump correctly with a rounded back.

Study the action of the pony's head and neck when jumping. On the approach his head will be slightly lowered. On take-off he shortens his neck, lifts his head and makes his spring with a rounded back and neck extended.

The rider's position must be watched all the time. Approaching in rising trot keeps your shoulders forward and takes your seat out of the saddle.

Subsequent cavaletti are done at the canter and until they have all been cleared the rider must maintain the forward position, shoulders forward, eyes looking ahead, seat just free of the saddle. The hip, knee and ankle must be springy to absorb the action of the jump: heels down, legs close to the pony's sides, and still. Hands follow the pony's head. The ideal to aim at is a light contact in a straight line from the bit, through the rein and on up to the rider's elbow.

The object of jumping at this stage is not to aim for height but to teach the rider to be confident, to stay in balance and not to interfere with his pony. For your pony it will also be a confidence stage, at which he will learn to be supple, obedient and self reliant. A pony that jumps well shows a high standard of training and ability.

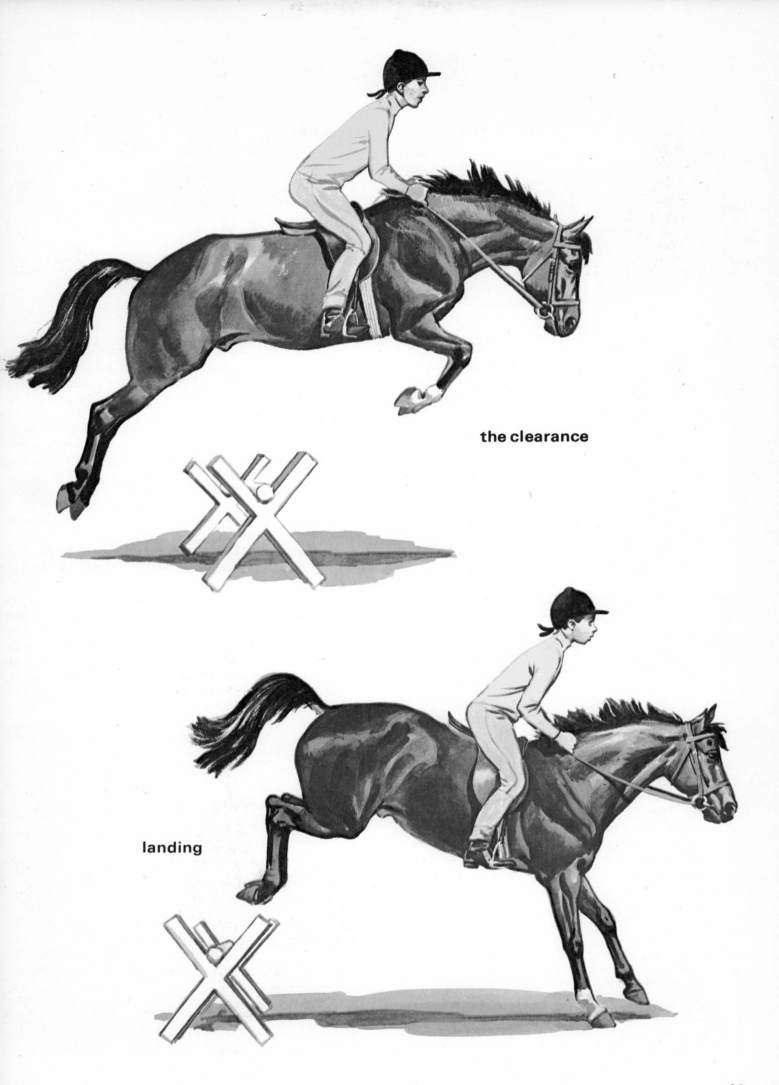

the clearance

landing

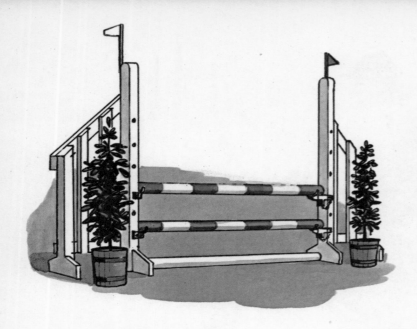

FENCES AND COURSES

A 'BOX' OF CAVALETTI

Once you can negotiate a line of cavaletti at varying distances you must begin to learn to guide and control your pony round a simple course. One of the best ways of doing this is to construct a 'box' of cavaletti as shown in the illustration on page 30. A single rider or several riders can work at it.

First circle round the markers at a trot. Next quietly incline through the gaps without changing pace. Pay attention to correct turns, riding straight and changing rein frequently.

Now do the same exercise at a trot, eventually taking the cavaletti in your stride and jumping quietly from every direction and coming back to a trot after each pair of jumps. The rider must concentrate on sitting still, doing as little as possible. Guide, control and regulate your pony's pace without kicking, pushing or pulling.

CONSTRUCTING A COURSE OF JUMPS

The 'box' of cavaletti can soon be developed into a course by adding small fences so that there are various changes of direction. The pace between fences should be the trot, with one or two canter strides before each fence, then back to a trot. Your pony will learn to be calm and obedient if this method of training is practised carefully. He should not be allowed to canter a course until he is calm and responsive at the trot.

FENCES: TEACHING THE PONY TO THINK

Fences can now be varied. Introduce your pony to cross rails, sleepers, logs, small brush fences and coloured walls. But remember that all schooling jumps must be solid; flimsy jumps can be dangerous. Your pony will have no respect for them if he thinks he can knock them over without trouble. Thin poles are dangerous; they break easily and can cause injury. It is therefore better to learn to jump with a few really well-made fences than with a large number of flimsy ones.

Your practice jumps should not be more than two feet to two feet six inches high to begin with. Increase the *spread* of the fences before you increase their *height*. This will encourage your pony to round his back and use his neck correctly, as already described.

Learn to space your fences so that your pony will be forced to jump with a different number of canter strides in between. This will teach him to think and to learn to adjust his stride before taking off. At the same time it will also help you to develop an 'eye' for the stride.

Always remember that the approach is the most important part of the jump. Once you have got the balance and pace right, you should interfere with the pony as little as possible. Keep your legs still and close to the pony's sides — but always ready to be used if needed. Your hands should be in light contact with a nicely stretched rein.

Preparing for a low jump. 1. place a cavaletto 18 inches high about 8 feet from the last in your line of trotting poles. Bring your pony in quietly at the trot. 2. Add a second cavaletto about 15 feet from the first and repeat the manoeuvre, allowing the pony to canter between the two jumps. 3. Put two cavaletti together to make a spread fence about two feet six inches wide. 4. Finally remove the poles one by one until your pony is jumping quietly and in a balanced manner without any poles at all.

A course of low practice jumps teaches your pony to think. Keep the jumps low. If you overface the pony with high fences at this stage he may well lose his confidence and his enthusiasm for jumping.

RIDING IN THE OPEN

The object of obtaining obedience and accuracy in your manege or school is to ensure that your pony is a light and pleasant ride outside, and you should try to combine work in the manege and riding in the open from the beginning.

In the early stages go in the company of an older horse or pony — one that is steady in traffic and will not get excited. Keep the pace to a walk to begin with. Until your pony can walk across open fields, over rough ground, and up and down hills he should not be allowed to go any faster. This quiet training pays in the long run, producing a pleasant and quiet pony that will go at the pace you want.

In the open it is advisable to ride with stirrups one or two holes shorter than used in the manege. This does not affect your position to any great extent but it enables you to sit lightly, which is essential when you are riding at faster paces and over long distances.

Continue to ride on straight lines when in the open. Do not allow your pony to wander about, otherwise he will pick up bad habits that will be hard to break, and all the good work put into training him will be lost. When riding up and down hill and over rough ground your shoulders should be in front of your hips.

Let your pony pick his way cautiously through shallow water—especially the first time he is expected to do so. If he refuses to ford the stream dismount and lead him in hand to give him confidence.

For riding over rough country, shorten your stirrup leathers one or two holes. To begin with keep the pace to a walk and concentrate on riding a straight course, without allowing the pony to wander about in all directions. Shoulders should be in front of your hips when riding up and down hill.

Keep a sharp look out for low branches in wooded areas.

THE GALLOP

This pace must be calm and controlled. We have said in a previous chapter that it is achieved by extending the canter. This must be done gradually over a longish distance to avoid excitement and any tendency to pull. At this pace on a free-going pony the rider's body will be forward, with the seat bones out of the saddle to allow complete freedom to the pony's back and loins. The rider's back must be flat with head up, riding 'in balance' and not hanging on to the pony's mouth. Practise maintaining an even pace across country over all types of ground, keeping the pony balanced between hand and leg.

At the basic paces of walk, trot and canter the rider's weight is mainly on the seat bones, but when riding across country at the faster paces on a free-going horse the rider must learn to ride lightly.

At the gallop therefore the rider's weight will be more on the ball of the foot and less on the seat. The rider's body will be further forward with the seat bones just clear of the saddle, the stirrup leathers will be vertical and the rider will be in balance by virtue of the shoulders being forward, and the hip, knee and ankle joint taking up the play of the movement.

As in the canter the pony swings his head, and the rider's head must allow this natural movement to take place. If the rider 'hangs on' to the pony's mouth, he will impede the movement and cause the pony to lean on the bit, which will eventually harden the mouth and encourage him to pull.

At all paces the rider's body and hands must conform to the pony's movement to allow the paces to develop naturally and easily. Of course, if the pony is not going freely forward then the rider must sit firmly on the seat bones, so that the rider's legs can be used to drive the pony into the desired speed; this should rarely be necessary on a generous pony that is well trained.

Aim at suppleness and obedience at the slower paces first, before attempting the gallop.

Exercises such as lengthening and shortening the stride at the trot, then later at the canter, will make your pony supple and obedient, and prepare him for work across country. He should not be made to gallop until suppleness is achieved at the trot and canter. Practice at these paces will produce a light and pleasant ride in all your future competition work.

ROAD SENSE

Horses and riders on the open road proceed in the same direction as the traffic, that is, on the left-hand side in countries where traffic drives on the left *(above)* and on the right-hand side where it drives on the right *(below)*.

Rules of the road vary from country to country but their aim is always the same: safety and courtesy for all road users. And they apply to horses and their riders just as much as to other traffic.

No pony should be ridden on a road until the rider is certain of two things: the rules of the road and the complete obedience of the pony.

Few drivers expect to find horses or ponies riding along their route, and fewer still understand how easily a horse or pony can be unnerved by the sight or sound of a moving vehicle. It is therefore up to the rider to be alert, trying to spot any situation or object likely to make the pony nervous before they actually come face to face with it.

Wherever there are grass verges, ride on them (unless of course they are private). Where there are no verges, keep well in to the side of the road. Ride with the reins shorter than usual so that you have greater control if the pony should be nervous. And keep to a slow, *controlled* pace – never anything faster than a *slow trot*. Take extra care on bends, where you can neither see nor be seen.

When riding in a group, proceed in single file with the first and last riders being responsible for giving signals if the cavalcade intends to turn left or right across the traffic.

As the evening light fades you become an even bigger hazard on the road. So ride with a stirrup light fixed to the side nearest the traffic, showing red to the rear and white to the front.

Acknowledge any courtesies shown by other road users with a smile (and a raised hand if you are in good control).

Riding in the country brings its own rules. Riders brought up in the country will be familiar with them but town riders will have to learn the country code: even wide open spaces may be private, and permission should be obtained before riding across fields. A gate is a barrier as private as any front door; a field or wood as private as a garden. Gates must be shut securely when the last rider passes through, and great care must be taken not to ride over seeded land or through growing crops. No rider should enter a field where sheep or cows might be frightened by the intrusion.

Avoid riding through fields where grazing sheep and cows might be alarmed by your intrusion.

SADDLERY

by Elwyn Hartley Edwards

Saddlery should be chosen because it is practical and not just because a particular item has become 'fashionable' because it has been worn (for some very good reason) by the horse of a show jumping star seen on television.

SADDLES

Comfort is most important when choosing a saddle: comfort for the pony and for the rider. A good saddle helps the rider to sit centrally so that he is in balance with the movement of his pony, and helps him to keep this position at all paces. It follows therefore that a saddle that has a seat with a fairly pronounced dip will be better for this purpose than one with a flatter seat. A flat seat is no help at all, since unless the rider is physically very strong, he is almost certain to sit on the back of the saddle and be behind the movement of his pony as well as receiving the full thrust of the hindquarters on his seat. This is uncomfortable for the pony and the rider, and much more tiring for him.

A comfortable, well-designed saddle will not make you ride well but it will help. It should not be too broad in the waist as this forces the thighs apart. And the stirrup bars should be placed so that they do not dig into the inside of the leg. Great thick stirrup leathers with big, clumsy buckles should be avoided; a width of $\frac{7}{8}$ inch is quite strong enough and not nearly so bulky under your leg.

GIRTHS

Buy a girth that is the right size for your pony. String or nylon is very satisfactory. The buckles should fasten just behind the crook of your leg. If the girth is too long the buckles will get under your leg, and if it is too short they will prevent you from using your leg comfortably and effectively.

STIRRUP IRONS

For your own safety buy stirrup irons that are big enough to allow your feet to slip out if you should happen to fall, but not so big that your foot can slip right through.

A SADDLE TO FIT THE PONY

Even if the saddle is as comfortable as an armchair it is no good at all if it doesn't fit the pony. First check it to make sure that the front arch is well clear of the withers and that the 'points' of the tree (the continuations of the arch) are wide enough. If they are not, the pony will be pinched and become sore. On the other hand, if the tree is too wide and presses on the wither that area will become sore. In both cases the pony will be reluctant to move freely, and particularly to jump, because every movement will cause him pain.

Next check that the cantle of the saddle is well clear of the pony's backbone and that the channel dividing the panel is nicely open so that there is no chance of it pressing against the easily damaged vertebrae of the spine. The spine must not be subjected to any pressure at any point along the whole length of the saddle.

SADDLE CARE

Keep your saddle clean and in good repair. Always remove sweat marks and check that the panel is smooth and free from lumps which, again, can cause sore places. A soft, supple saddle is more comfortable for you both.

THE BRIDLE

For the pony to be really comfortable the bridle must fit properly. The *bit* of a well-fitting bridle hangs exactly level in the mouth, just high enough to cause

a slight wrinkle to the corners of the lips. Too high it will cause discomfort, and too low it may knock against the teeth, or encourage the pony to put his tongue over the bit, which is a bad habit.

The *browband* should be plenty big enough, so that it cannot pull the headpiece forward against the pony's ears, which would irritate him and make him throw his head about. And — very important — the *throat latch* must be loose enough to allow the insertion of at least two fingers. If the throat latch is fitted too tightly or is too short, the pony cannot flex at the poll and carry his head well — which is not surprising considering that he is being throttled.

To complete the pony's comfort the bridle needs to be cleaned regularly and kept soft and supple with the regular use of saddle soap and an occasional application of oil or a grease like Kocholine. Hard, stiff, dirty leather is not comfortable and can make the pony's head sore, particularly the sensitive areas behind the ears.

A *neck strap* is a useful article of saddlery which is not used often enough. It is an ordinary strap round the pony's neck just in front of the saddle. If you hold on to it with one hand when you are jumping in an awkward place and when you are riding up and down hill it will save your pony's mouth from unnecessary pulling.

CLEANING

The saddle and bridle should always be hung up correctly when not in use, with the saddle on a special saddle bracket to avoid distortion or damage to the tree.

For cleaning the saddle should be placed on a saddle horse, and the bridle on a cleaning hook.

With the stirrup irons removed and buckles on the bridle undone, apply saddle soap to all surfaces (inside and out) with a damp sponge. Do not use too much soap, and rub it well in.

Buckles should be rubbed clean with a dry cloth, and stirrup irons and bits washed and thoroughly dried. All stitching — particularly on the stirrup leathers and girth — must be examined carefully and frequently. Good leather lasts for many years but stitching can rot quite quickly.

Two pieces of advice can never be given too often: never use *hot* water on saddlery, and never place the saddle near a fire or stove.

SADDLING UP

CARRYING

Carry the saddle with the front arch in the crook of your arm, and the bridle in the same hand.

There are four main points to watch when you fit a saddle: they should be checked with the rider actually sitting in the saddle.

1. The weight of the saddle and the rider must be evenly distributed over the pony's back, on both sides of the spine.

2. There must be no weight on the pony's loins.

3. The pony's spine and the withers must be completely free from any pressure.

4. The play of the pony's shoulder must not be restricted in any way.

SADDLING ROUTINE

Always tie your pony up with halter and rope before attempting any task. It saves time in the long run and it can be dangerous to have him loose while you saddle up or perform any other task.

1. Collect your saddle and bridle and neck strap. The stirrup irons should be run up on the leathers, and the girth attached on the off-side. Undo the throat latch and the noseband buckle.

2. Hang up your bridle and stand the saddle on end while securing the pony.

3. Smooth the coat and the girth place with your hands.

4. Standing on the near side, pick up the saddle by the front arch with your left hand, and with your right hand on the rear arch (or vice versa if you saddle from the off-side).

5. Place the saddle firmly on the pony's back, well forward on the withers, then slide it back into its proper position. This is to ensure that the hair lies flat. The point of the saddle should fit snugly behind the top of the shoulder.

6. Make sure that the sweat flaps and girth straps are flat on the near-side. Walk round to the front of the pony and see that all is flat on the other side.

7. Let the girth down and buckle it gently and with sufficient tightness to hold it in place. Make certain that the skin is not wrinkled behind the elbow.

8. Now slide the halter round his neck and put on the bridle.

The bridle: 1. headpiece. 2. browband. 3. throat latch. 4. noseband. 5. snaffle bit. 6. reins. 7. cheekpiece.

The saddle: 1. cantle. 2. seat. 3. waist. 4. pommel. 5. stirrup bars under skirt. 6. flap. 7. stirrup leather. 8. girth. 9. stirrup iron. 10. skirt. 11. panel.

FITTING THE BRIDLE

1. Hold the bridle in the left hand with the browband towards the elbow, and the headpiece and reins in the palm of your hand.

2. Place the reins over the pony's back and neck.

3. With your right hand take hold of the headpiece.

4. Slide your left hand over the pony's muzzle, holding the bridle close to his forehead with the other.

5. Take the bit in your left hand and hold it against the pony's lips. At the same time push your fingers between the lips. This will make your pony open his mouth for the bit.

6. Slide the headpiece over the ears and adjust with both hands.

7. Do up all buckles and tuck the straps through their keepers.

8. Stand in front and see that browband and noseband are level. Adjust the bit if necessary, counting the holes on each side to ensure that it is level.

9. Undo the halter and hang it up when you lead out.

HOW TO OFF SADDLE

1. Stand on the near-side of the pony and before removing the saddle, take the reins over his head and slip the ends in the crook of your arm nearest his head.

2. Raise the saddle flap and undo the girth, lowering it gently with the left hand on the front arch.

3. Slide the saddle off towards you and catch the girth in your right hand. Place it with the inside down over the saddle seat.

4. Stand the saddle down carefully and well away from the pony.

5. Run your hand over the back and girth place to check for any signs of injury or rubbing.

REMOVING THE BRIDLE

1. Replace the reins over the neck, and strap a halter or head collar round the pony's neck.

2. Unbuckle the throat latch and noseband.

3. Take the reins, headpiece and neckstrap in your right hand, and place your left on the pony's face above the nostrils.

4. Slip the reins, headpiece and neckstrap over the ears, and gently allow the pony to ease the bit out of his mouth.

5. Hang the bridle over your left arm and put on a halter if you wish to secure the pony.

6. Take the saddle and bridle immediately to the saddle room and hang them up.

When you are mounted check the stirrup length and adjust if necessary, holding the reins in your right hand and looking ahead so that you are in control if the pony moves.

GROOMING A STABLED PONY

by Bill Lithgow

A complete grooming kit consists of:

A hoof pick—for cleaning out the feet.

A dandy brush—for removing dust, heavy dirt and caked mud.

A body brush—to remove scurf and dust from the coat, mane and tail.

A curry comb—made of metal or rubber, for cleaning the body brush.

A water brush—used damp on the mane, tail and feet.

A stable sponge—for cleaning eyes, muzzle and dock.

A wisp—made of hay or straw and used for improving circulation and massage.

A stable rubber—a cloth for giving the final glossy polish after grooming.

The stabled pony is unable to roll and exercise at will as he can in his natural state. So grooming is necessary to keep him healthy and in condition. It helps to prevent disease, ensures cleanliness and improves his appearance (something every proud rider is interested in).

GROOMING ROUTINES

These are the main routines to be carried out regularly:

Feet: first tie up your pony and then pick out his feet, checking while you do so that the shoes are secure and in good order.

Body: brush with the dandy brush to remove caked dirt and sweat marks, but avoiding the tender parts.

Next take the body brush and thoroughly brush out the mane. Then, with short circular strokes and leaning your weight on the brush, go all over the body. After every four or five strokes draw the brush sharply across the curry comb to remove grease and dirt. Tap the comb on the floor to clean it.

Next gently do the head and, finally, the tail — taking care not to break the hairs.

Now take the wisp, dampen it and bring it down vigorously with a smack on those parts where the muscles are hard and flat. This stimulates the skin, improves the circulation, and brings a shine to the coat.

Head: with a damp sponge clean out the eyes, muzzle, nostrils and dock. 'Lay' the mane in its correct direction with a damp water brush.

Finishing off: wash and oil the feet and finally go all over with the rubber to remove the last traces of dirt.

If it is cold, keep your pony partially covered with rugs while grooming him.

1. dandy brush. 2. water brush. 3. body brush. 4. stable sponge. 5. hoof pick. 6. mane and tail comb. 7. curry comb. 8. quick-release knot for tethering.

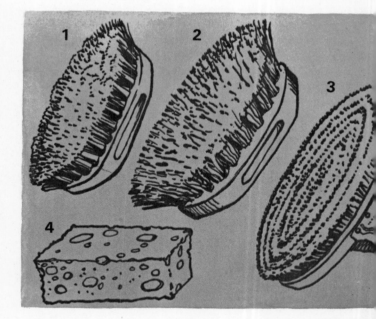

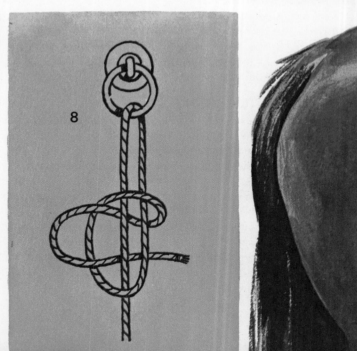

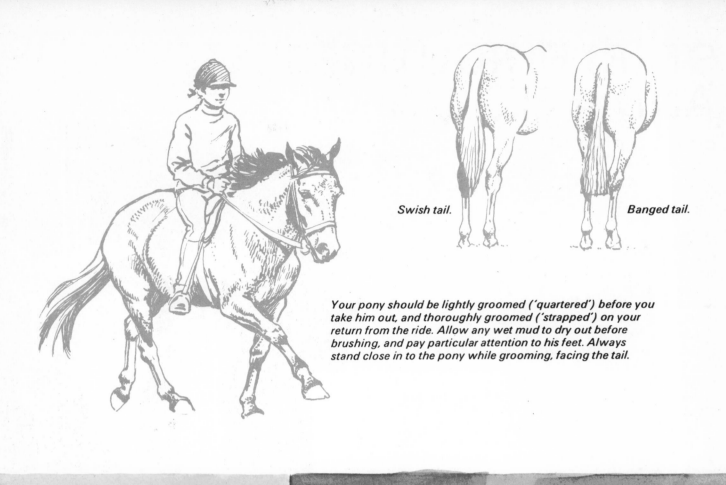

Swish tail.

Banged tail.

Your pony should be lightly groomed ('quartered') before you take him out, and thoroughly groomed ('strapped') on your return from the ride. Allow any wet mud to dry out before brushing, and pay particular attention to his feet. Always stand close in to the pony while grooming, facing the tail.

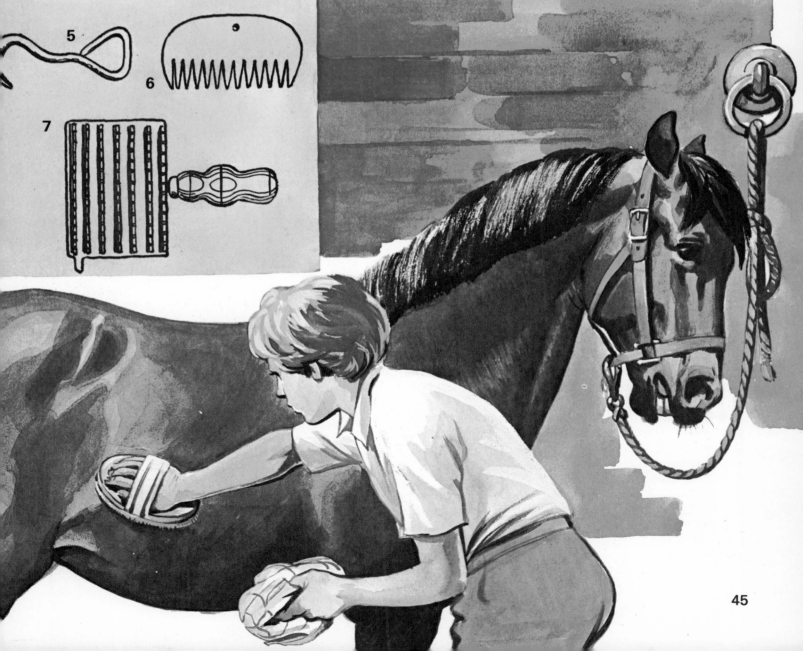

STABLE ROUTINES AND FEEDING

by Bill Lithgow

STABLING

Good ventilation and drainage are essential in a stable. The ponies should be kept warm with extra clothing (rugs, etc.) not by a stuffy atmosphere. The floor should be slightly sloping to allow water to drain away but should not be slippery.

Loose boxes are better than stalls because they allow the ponies free movement. For a horse a loose box not less than 14 feet by 12 feet is needed, and for a pony not less than 12 feet by 10.

Stalls are space-savers but ponies that are kept tethered get bored and boredom produces all sorts of bad habits (like crib biting).

Swinging bails can also be used as divisions but care has to be taken to see that they are hung high enough to prevent the ponies getting their legs over them. The bails must also be fixed in such a way that they can be released quickly if necessary. Although swinging bails allow the ponies to remain untethered they give no protection against bullying or neck biting.

CLOTHING

Woollen, hemp or jute rugs kept in place with a breast strap and roller keep the pony warm at night. Cotton sweat rugs and sheets are also frequently used.

New Zealand rugs made of waterproof material are invaluable when ponies are turned out.

BEDDING

All stabled ponies should be given a clean bed, well banked up at the sides for extra protection.
Straw: wheat straw is best but 'combined' barley is also good. If oat straw is used the ponies are apt to eat it.
Deep litter: this is the method of removing only the soiled parts of the straw each day and adding new straw to replace it.
Shavings and sawdust: these are both clean and comfortable but are not easy to dispose of.
Peat moss: this makes a good bed but is inclined to be dusty.

Whatever material is used for the bed, all damp and soiled patches have to be removed daily if the pony is to remain healthy.

FEEDING AND WATERING

The pony in his natural state eats most of the time and a little at a time. So when he is stabled we must try to keep as near to natural patterns as possible but adjusting the food according to the amount of work the pony is going to do. The first rule must be, then, to

Picking up a fore leg: face the tail and gently slide the hand nearest the pony down his shoulder to the back of the leg. Gently squeeze the back tendons and when your hand reaches the fetlock, say 'Up'.

Picking up a hind leg: again stand close in facing the tail and run the hand nearest the pony down to the hock and inside the cannon bone. Squeeze the back tendons gently and give the order 'Up' as you are about to lift the leg.

feed 'little and often', with plenty of bulk food such as hay.

The pony needs more protein because he is doing extra work. The best grain for horses is oats, but they usually make a pony 'hot-up' and difficult to manage so the modern substitute for oats is horse and pony nuts. Nuts contain all the right ingredients to keep your pony fit. They are clean, easy to feed, easy to look after, and they never vary in quality. Combined with good hay for bulk most ponies will do well on these two items of food and nothing else.

But some variety is essential: so a few sliced carrots occasionally helps his digestion.

Damp bran adds bulk to feeds and also aids digestion. And because ponies like sweet things, sugar beet pulp and molasses are always welcome.

Linseed is very warming and good for the coat in the winter months. It should be soaked and boiled until it forms a jelly, then allowed to cool. Feed it with the evening meal—about 4 ounces is sufficient for one pony.

Your pony needs to be fed at least three times a day and the feeding times must be regular. He must also have access to a bucket of clean water at all times so that he may drink whenever he wishes.

CLIPPING

Under natural conditions the pony's thick winter coat provides him with a warm covering when the weather is cold and food scarce. The natural greasiness in the hair keeps the warmth in and helps the pony to maintain condition.

But this thick coat is a drawback when we wish to work the pony; it makes him sweat excessively, and it prevents rapid drying after exertion. A clipped pony on the other hand can work without distress, can work faster and longer, dries more quickly, is easier to clean and is less likely to develop skin diseases.

WHEN TO CLIP
Ponies vary considerably in the thickness of their coats. Some thoroughbred fine-haired ponies need possibly one clip a year, whereas thick-coated ponies may need three or more clips. But early autumn when the coat grows thick and rather dull is the time for the first clip. The last clip of the year depends on when the new spring coat starts to come through, but should not be delayed later than February.

HOW TO CLIP
Modern electric clipping machines are easy to use after a little practice, but adult assistance is needed to begin with. The pony must be dry and cool, and you must allow plenty of time for the job. The tender spots are the ears, head and belly, and great care and patience are required to keep your pony quiet as you clip them. On no account must the insides of the ears be clipped.

Care must also be taken not to clip the root of the tail or the sides of the mane.

Allow your pony to feed from a haynet when you are clipping him, and cover up the parts you have clipped with a warm blanket to keep him warm.

TYPES OF CLIP
There are various types of clip, as you can see from the illustrations, but the hunter clip is the most practical if your pony is going to be worked hard.

Unclipped: natural coat left to grow.

Trace clip: hair removed from the belly and sometimes from the underside of the neck.

Hunter clip: clipped out but with saddle marks and legs left unclipped.

Full clip: natural coat growth removed.

TRIMMING

Trimming is the operation to remove untidy hair from the legs, body, mane and tail. Trimming scissors and a steel tail comb are the equipment needed.

Skilful use of the scissors on the back tendons and round the coronet of a hairy pony will make his appearance much smarter, though on some breeds of pony this hair should not be touched.

The trimming scissors may also be used to remove the fine hairs on the edge of the ears.

The mane can be made neat and tidy by careful pulling. The long hairs are pulled out from underneath a few at a time, after being separated with the tail comb. Careful pulling will also reduce the mane to the required length. Some ponies' manes are very thick and unmanageable and are clipped right off. This is called 'hogging'.

Plaiting is also a neat way of showing off your pony. Much practice is needed to make a good job of it. First damp the whole mane with a water brush then divide the mane into the number of plaits you require (6 or 7, and one on the forelock). Plait each division and, near the end of each, plait in a rubber band or piece of thread. Then turn the plait underneath in a roll, or loop the rubber band tightly over the whole plait.

Tails are also tidied and kept neat by careful pulling of the long hairs at the side. But many people nowadays prefer to plait their ponies' tails, and it is a much easier operation than pulling. The method is to plait the long outside hairs together so that you have one long plait down the centre of the dock. A long tail collects mud and should therefore be kept a reasonable length by 'banging' (cutting) the bottom with the trimming scissors.

The tail should be washed with warm water and ordinary soap at frequent intervals to remove excessive grease and scurf. Rinse in clean water after washing.

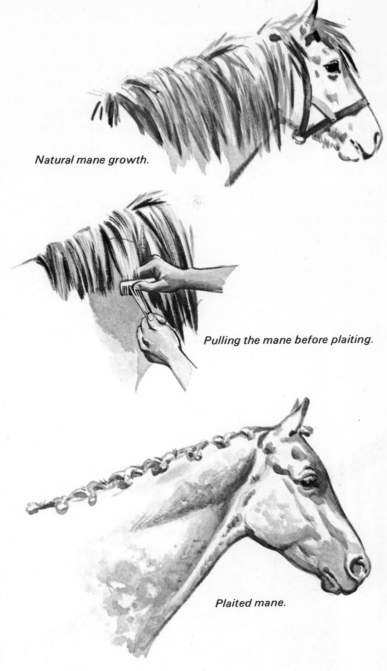

Natural mane growth.

Pulling the mane before plaiting.

Plaited mane.

Hogged mane: natural growth cut very short.

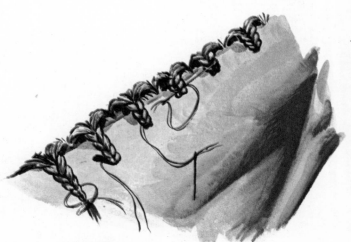

Sewing up the plaits.

A pony that is turned out to grass instead of being stabled lives a much more natural life and as a result is fitter, healthier and happier. There are also some advantages for the owner too: less attention is required and therefore caring for the pony takes up less time. Grass-kept ponies exercise themselves enough for health but not enough for fitness.

The grass-kept pony feeds more naturally. There is also less danger of him suffering injury to wind and limb because he is in better physical condition to stand up to any work given to him.

There are of course some snags in keeping your pony at grass: he will not be as readily available when wanted as a stabled pony — and he may be some distance away, perhaps even wet and dirty. Added to this he may even be difficult to catch — though with proper care this can be avoided.

Ponies kept permanently at grass or under the combined system should be given protective New Zealand rugs if they are clipped. And if a grass-kept pony is brought in only for the night before and (perhaps) after hunting, showing or rallies, make sure that there is plenty of air in the stables.

THE FIELD AND THE FENCING

A grass-kept pony needs at least an acre of grass in good condition. Ideally the field should be securely fenced, reasonably well drained, and provided with a constant water supply, some shade and preferably an open-fronted shed for shelter.

Post and rail fencing is the best but expensive. Second best is natural thorn, and after that plain wire (which must be taut and its lowest strand at least one foot off the ground to prevent the ponies getting their feet over it). Barbed wire hurdles and chestnut palings are fencings to be avoided.

When expense is no matter, electric fencing has a great advantage: it is very efficient and can be moved about very easily. It gives the ponies a slight and quite harmless shock whenever they touch the wire surrounding the area in which they have been enclosed.

FIELD CARE

Ponies are wasteful grazers. In their search for the juiciest, most palatable shoots they will trample down grass that is perfectly good, and parts of the

THE GRASS-KEPT PONY

by Bill Lithgow

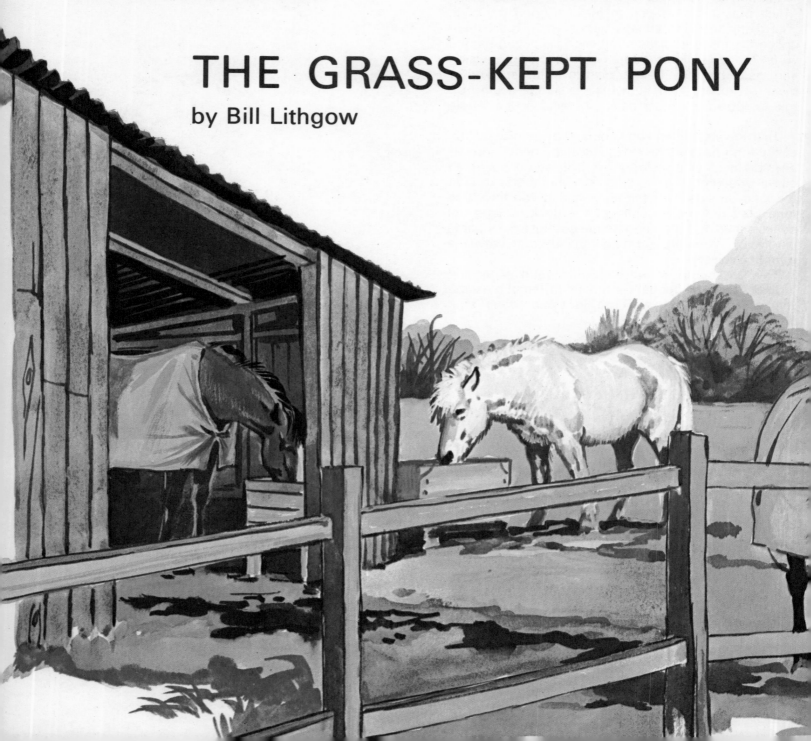

field become so stained with droppings that the grass is no longer suitable for grazing.

Dividing the area so that the ponies can be moved from one part to another while the grazed parts freshen up, removing droppings regularly wherever possible, dressing the field with fertilizer every few years, and keeping the parts that the ponies don't eat cut (or grazed by cows or sheep) are some of the ways of preserving the condition of the grass.

FEEDING
In late autumn, winter and early spring there is little good in the grass, so hay and — depending on the work being done — oats, nuts, etc. has to be given as well. The feed should be put where the ponies normally shelter.

A grass-kept pony that is being worked, usually needs more food than a stabled pony because of the effect of the cold — a hungry pony is a cold pony.

In summer when the grass is rich some ponies get far too fat. This is bad for them and makes them uncomfortable to ride, and they should either be kept on a fairly bare area or shut up in a shed or stable for part of the day to keep them away from the grass.

EXERCISE
Bringing a grass-kept pony to fitness requires as much work as from a stabled one in the first place. But once in full work — hunting, pony club rallies, jumping, hacking and so on — it will give itself sufficient exercise in between whiles.

GROOMING
Remember that the natural grease in the pony's coat helps to keep out wet and cold. So do not groom too thoroughly. It is enough to remove the mud, sweat marks and stains.

ROUTINE
1. Inspect the ponies daily for injury and general condition.

2. Give the ponies a titbit every time you inspect them. This will make them readier to allow themselves to be caught when you want them. Some ponies are ready enough to approach you but move off as soon as you try to put something on them. These are best turned out in a fitted headcollar.

3. Except in very severe weather one or two feeds a day should be sufficient, and they are probably most conveniently given night and morning.

4. Like all animals, ponies appreciate a settled daily routine, but since the reason for keeping them at grass is often because the owner has other things to do, there is no need to be a slave to this.

THE COMBINED SYSTEM
This is really the best system: the pony is kept out by day, or part of it, and put in the stable at night. While this is more trouble for the owner, it overcomes the problems which occur when a pony is kept permanently at grass.

FEET AND SHOES

TAKING CARE OF THE PONY'S FEET

Unless your pony's feet are in good healthy condition he will keep falling lame not only in the foot but in other parts of the leg too. To keep his feet healthy you need to understand how they are made and how they are affected by shoeing.

Inside the foot there are sensitive structures which keep the insensitive parts healthy. The insensitive parts are in turn protected by the horny growths surrounding them. The hard, insensitive outer areas can be divided into three parts: the *wall*, the *sole* and the *frog*.

The wall is the part of the pony's foot that you can see when the foot is on the ground. It grows from the coronet in the same way that finger nails grow from a cuticle, and extends right round the foot to the heels, where it forms the *bars*. A healthy wall has a shine to it.

The sole grows from the sensitive structure inside the pony's foot. Although it is a hard substance it can be bruised by sharp stones or punctured by nails. A healthy sole is slightly concave.

The frog is a non-slipping device. It also absorbs some of the impact when the pony's foot comes to the ground. A healthy frog is essential for a healthy foot, and the cleft of the frog must receive particular attention when you pick out the feet.

SHOEING

In his natural state the pony was not shod, but when he has to work or travel on hard roads, shoes are needed. They protect his feet so long as certain rules are adhered to.

The wall of the pony's foot grows about half an inch every four to six weeks, so his shoes must be removed at least every six weeks to allow this growth to be cut off to give the correct level of the foot. Levelling the foot is the blacksmith's first duty. After the growth has been trimmed the same shoes may be replaced if they are not too worn.

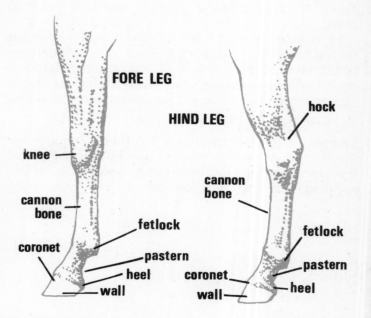

When your pony is being shod check these points:
1. The shoe fits the foot.
2. No rough edges should be left.
3. The toe clip must lie flat against the wall.
4. The clenches (the nail ends) must lie flat against the wall.
5. A light shoeing iron should be used.
6. The frog must be in contact with the ground.
7. No daylight must show between shoe and foot.
8. The nails must be driven home.
9. The heels of the shoe should be neither too long nor too short.

In addition to regular shoeing or refitting visits your pony will need immediate attention from the blacksmith if:
1. a shoe is loose
2. a shoe has worn thin
3. the clenches have risen and the nails are loose
4. a shoe has come off

There are many types of shoe but unless the blacksmith suggests otherwise an ordinary light hunter shoe serves most general purposes very well.

LAMENESS

Most ponies are fairly hardy but when lameness does occur the first thing to do is to find the lame leg, and then the cause of it.

To detect the lame leg, trot the pony slowly on the road. He will try to save the injured limb by putting more weight on the sound ones.

The next thing to look and feel for is heat, pain or swelling. Heat is always an indication of something wrong. It may indicate one of the following causes:

Pricked sole — *where a shoeing nail has actually penetrated the sensitive part of the foot.*

Nail binding — *a shoeing nail pressing against the sensitive part of the foot.*

Bruised sole — *bruising caused by a stone.*

Corns — *caused in the heel region by bad shoeing or ill-fitting shoes.*

Laminitis — *fever in the feet caused by too rich feeding. This often occurs in ponies when they are feeding on spring grass.*

All these conditions require expert treatment.

Your pony's joints and limbs should be clean and free from any swelling at all times. If there is any sign of swelling or heat on the back tendons or any joint, then seek adult advice right away.

Provided your pony is brought up to a fit state gradually by careful, slow exercise over a long period swellings, strains and sprains should not occur. But watch for the first sign of unlevel paces or unusual heat or swelling and take immediate action to find the cause.

The wall of the pony's hoof grows about half an inch every four to six weeks. This growth must be removed by the blacksmith at least every six weeks to give the correct foot level. The old shoes can then be refitted if they are not too worn, or new ones fitted.

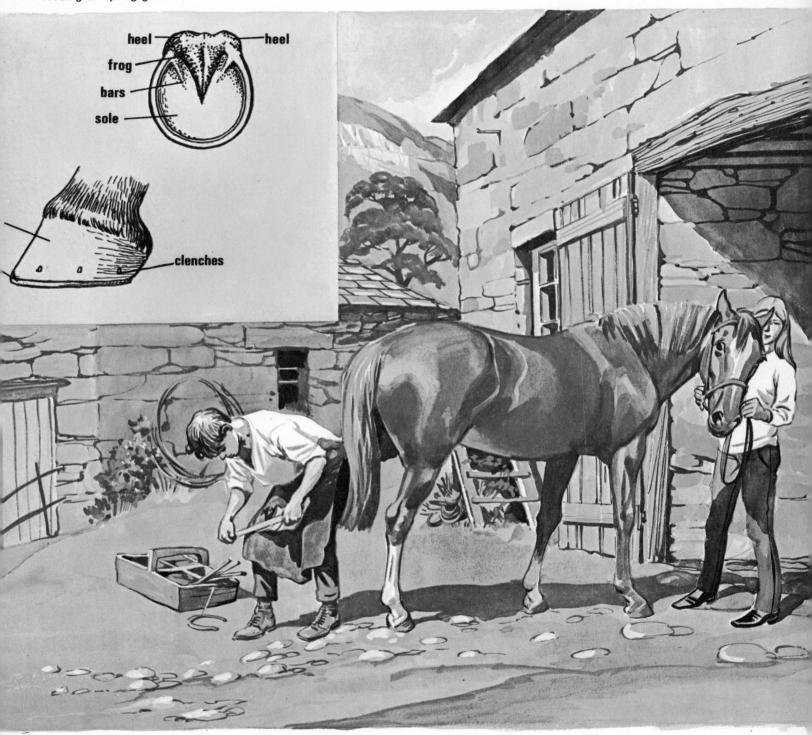

KEEPING YOUR PONY HEALTHY

All riders should be able to recognise the signs of good health in a pony.

His forefeet will always be firmly planted on the ground; he may rest a hindleg but never a foreleg unless there is something the matter with it.

The head is always on the alert, with eyes wide open and shining, ears pricking to and fro. The coat shines and the skin may be rolled about on the muscles underneath.

His breathing is easy and deep, his nostrils and lips clean, and his breath clear.

The dung passed by a healthy pony should be soft and without much smell. The urine should be clear.

A healthy pony will always be eager for his feed.

His paces will be level and he should move briskly.

Train yourself to look for these pointers to good health, and if you spot anything out of the ordinary, seek the advice of an adult or the vet.

You can keep your pony in regular good health by following these first essentials: a good routine of regular feeding, grooming, and exercise whether your pony is stabled or kept in a field.

SYMPTOMS OF COMMON AILMENTS

Colic: a pain in the stomach caused by irregular feeding or a sudden change of diet. *Symptoms*: the pony will not eat, is restless and tries to lie down. He also keeps looking round at his flanks. *Treatment*: keep him warm and try to make him eat a warm bran mash. Walk him round. If the symptoms last for more than an hour, send for the vet.

Simple fever: a rise in the body temperature above the normal 100°F (a pony's temperature is taken at the

Train yourself to look for the pointers to good health in your pony, and if you spot anything that seems out of the ordinary seek the advice of an adult or the vet. Never work a pony that you suspect is sick.

anus so adult help will usually be needed). *Symptoms*: the pony is off his feed, dull, listless and probably has a staring coat. *Treatment*: fevers can be the warning sign of many conditions, so keep the pony warmly covered in his stable and send for the vet.

Colds: various causes. *Symptoms*: discharges from the nose, and dull eyes. *Treatment*: stop working the pony, keep him warm and give him soft tempting feeds. 'Steam' his head once a day by putting hay into the bottom of a wide sack, adding a teaspoon of friar's balsam and pouring hot water on to it. Swing the bag round for a minute or two and then apply to the pony's muzzle. Ponies usually like this treatment and it helps to clear the head.

If the pony's temperature rises above 103°F, you should send for the vet.

Simple cough: this may be caused by dusty hay or a sore throat from a cold. *Treatment*: take the pony off work and feed him bran mashes and green food. Damp down the hay with a watering can, and rub the outside of his throat with a mild liniment. Small doses of a cough electuary (produced by the vet) will help to ease the irritation. If the cough persists, seek professional advice.

SKIN DISEASES

The commonest skin diseases are lice infection, ringworm and sweet itch.

Lice infection: long-coated animals at grass are prone to this. *Symptoms*: the pony's tail and mane are rubbed quite raw against gate posts or fences. *Treatment*: rub in a good lice powder obtainable from the chemists. To kill the eggs the pony must be clipped, and then singed with a special singeing lamp.

Sweet itch and ringworm: with sweet itch there is irritation and rubbing of the head, crest and withers.

With ringworm small patches of hair fall off the pony's body. This is a highly contagious skin complaint and should be treated by the vet.

There are many other pony ailments — too many to list here. But give your pony regular attention and you will avoid most of them. And when in doubt *seek advice*.

PREPARING FOR A SHOW

by Jennie Loriston-Clarke

Almost every pony rider has an ambition to compete at shows. While at national events the trophies usually go to 'show class' ponies, at local events every well-schooled and well-turned out pony that is ridden by a competent and well-turned out rider has a sporting chance of winning. What the judges are looking for in the junior classes is the combination of a fit, well-groomed, obedient and supple pony who responds to the aids of an accurate and considerate rider. Neat, precise combinations that carry out simple manoeuvres well will take home more rosettes than riders trying to perform manoeuvres that are too advanced for them, and on ponies too big and spirited for them.

LONG-TERM PLANS

Preparation for a show begins long before the date is announced. No pony shows to best advantage unless he is fit and well. So the first essential is to make sure that he is in good condition without being fat. This means that he must be properly cared for from the earliest possible moment. Regular exercise and schooling will keep his muscles well toned up.

Before entering shows he must be able to accept the bit nicely and go freely forward in a good even rhythm at walk, trot and canter. He must also be able to change rein and canter a figure of eight smoothly. In other words, he must be supple, obedient and responsive before you begin to think of showing him.

When you have decided that you are both ready to compete, find out what the entry regulations and class details of each show are. They are not necessarily identical for every show and it is wise to check beforehand from the organisers of the show that both you and the pony are qualified to enter the classes you choose.

PRE-SHOW TRAINING

Pre-show training should be carried out in the saddlery to be used at the show itself if possible. A well-fitting saddle, straight-cut to show off the pony's shoulders is ideal. If you are riding a novice pony you will be required to ride him in a snaffle bridle only. If your pony is not a novice, you can ride in either a double bridle or a pelham. But avoid using

excessively severe bits as these are liable to be penalised by the judges.

PRE-SHOW GROOMING

As you get nearer the show date you must think about trimming up the pony. His mane should be pulled short enough for plaiting (approximately four to six inches long). His tail should be pulled or, if preferred, it can be left as it is and plaited. It is a great advantage to trim your pony well by taking off the whiskers under his chin, and trimming his heels neatly. Do this either with a comb and scissors or *very carefully* with clippers.

THE DAY BEFORE THE SHOW

Make sure the pony's mane and tail are clean. If you are in any doubt, give them a good shampoo, rinsing them well so that no soap is left behind. Make sure that your earlier trimming is still neat. Tack must be spotlessly clean, and knee caps, a smart day rug, tail bandage, and possibly a stocking to put his tail in to keep it clean while travelling should be laid ready for use. The head collar should be checked for cleanness.

THE DAY OF THE SHOW
by Jennie Loriston-Clarke

WHAT TO WEAR

The rider must be as correctly turned out as the pony. For young competitors a hard velvet cap or bowler, a neatly fitting shirt with a collar and tie, a navy blue or black coat, gloves (preferably dark in colour), neat-fitting jodhpurs, and jodhpur boots are correct. It is also quite correct to wear top boots but these are very expensive and are not necessary for this kind of showing. You should also carry a show cane.

It goes without saying that extra care should be taken to make sure that tack is neat and correctly fitted.

THE DAY OF THE SHOW

Feed the pony early, then go and kit yourself up. To keep your jodhpurs and shirt clean, put a pair of jeans and an overall over the top. Then return to the pony and plait up his mane with very neat plaits (preferably about eight to ten). The illustrations on page 49 show how. Then bandage him up and take him to the show in good time.

ARRIVAL AT THE SHOW

When you arrive take your pony around the show ground to let him get the feel of it. Give him enough work to do so that he does not appear too fresh in the show ring. Plan to be ready ten minutes before your class is due and start putting the finishing touches to the pony three-quarters of an hour beforehand.

Remove the bandages. If he has white legs rub a little chalk block into the white hair, brushing it briskly off afterwards. Put a little Vaseline round his muzzle and eyes, give him a good brush over, and finish him off with a stable rubber. Brush out his tail, apply his hoof oil, and set diamond squares on his quarters (this is done with a little comb about an inch and a half in diameter).

At this point you are ready to start tidying yourself up: put on your coat, tidy your hair back (into a net preferably if you are a girl), put your competition number and gloves on. Collect your show cane. You and your pony are ready to face the judges.

Make certain that you know the rules for any particular competition.

Think about your pony during the day. See that he gets a short drink immediately after showing, and loosen girths whenever possible.

Don't sit about on his back and don't gallop about unnecessarily. Shelter him from sun or wind, and lead him round until he has cooled off after showing.

If you feed him during the day make certain that he has time to digest it.

When the day is over, make your pony comfortable for the journey home, and before leaving, try to find the secretary of the show or one of the organisers and thank them for an enjoyable day.

If you cannot find a litter bin, take away with you any litter you may have.

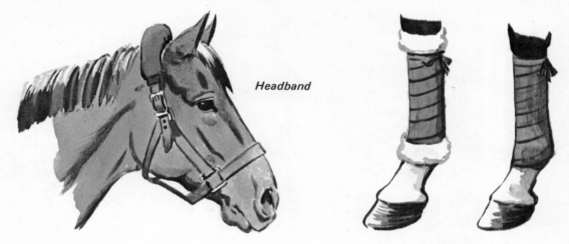

Headband

Working and stable bandages

PROTECTING YOUR PONY

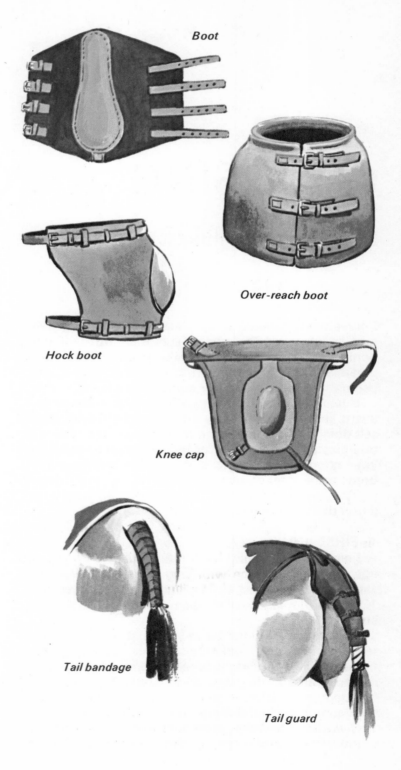

Boot

Over-reach boot

Hock boot

Knee cap

Tail bandage

Tail guard

Your pony's legs are most vulnerable to injury. These injuries can occur when travelling, in the stable or when being ridden. So boots and bandages of various types should be kept for protection when necessary.

A set of warm woollen stable bandages is the first essential. Carefully applied they keep your pony warm when travelling and protect him from blows and knocks. In the stable they can be used for warmth after a hard day or support if he has had an injury.

Elasticated bandages made of stockinette can be used for exercise; with gamjee or cotton wool underneath they give good support to weak tendons. On a normal pony they should not be necessary.

Any bandage carelessly put on can be a source of danger and injury.

There are various types of boots that can be used when schooling a pony to protect his shins but they are rarely necessary under normal circumstances. The most common injury is caused by 'brushing'. This is when one foot strikes against the inside fetlock of the other leg. Brushing boots can then be used until the wound is healed but the cause of the brushing must be removed.

Over-reach boots prevent serious injury when a pony strikes into his foreleg with a hind shoe.

Brushing and over reaching can often be cured by good shoeing.

Protection of the head is sometimes necessary and can be achieved by rolling a bandage round the top of the halter.

The tail should always be protected by a bandage or tail guard when travelling.

CHOOSING A PONY

by Jennifer Williams

Ponies often have an uncanny way of summing their owners up before the owners sum them up! Different ponies suit different riders. Like people, their temperaments vary and it's hard to alter this. That is why certain horses go better for some than others.

Buying a pony is an exciting – and expensive – event and if you are lucky enough ever to find yourself doing so, it is important to decide on the essential qualities you are looking for before you actually make your choice. For example, if you are buying a first pony there are certain priorities to be considered which you may not need to take into account later if you buy a second pony.

A FIRST PONY

A first pony is usually for a rider under ten years of age so you don't want anything more than 12·2 h.h. (and for a rider under eight preferably not bigger than 12 h.h.). Ponies smaller than this tend to be less strong.

The qualities to look for in your first pony are good temperament and willingness. This last is sometimes missing in certain breeds. For a beginner it is most important to get a good start to riding so a 'schoolmaster' type is better than a young pony – two learners don't make easy progress together.

Make sure that any pony you think of buying has a good mouth and is not too thick in the neck. Ponies with badly put on necks and thick through can be pullers, and no young rider is strong enough to cope with a puller.

At this stage your legs are fairly short and you will find a narrow pony is easier to sit on than a very broad one!

The breed you choose is purely a matter of personal preference. Every rider has likes and dislikes. But a good first choice would be a pure Mountain Welsh, for on the whole the breed has most to offer a young rider: they are attractive to look at, and on the whole have good riding fronts, ideal size and the best of temperaments.

Other small British native breeds are the Shetland, the Exmoor and the Dartmoor – the latter being extremely popular. And of course there are dozens of ponies that are cross-bred, and excellent they can be. If you do have the good fortune to be able to buy a pony, it is useful to know its breeding when you buy it, if only for registration purposes.

A SECOND PONY

If you ever reach the point of buying a *second* pony there are many things to be taken into account. The most important is to decide what price you are willing to pay, what facilities you can offer it, and how much time you will have to care for it. It is no good buying a real quality pony, for example, if you haven't got time to look after it or good conditions to keep it in.

INSPECTING A PONY
The first thing to do when you inspect a pony is to have a look at it without the saddle on. Then ask the owner to ride it and see it through all its paces before getting on it yourself. Next have it led up in-hand at the walk and trot on a good hard, flat surface to see how it moves from the side and from behind. Then test out its temperament; make sure you can manage it in a large field and not just an indoor school. A traffic-proof pony is a 'must' these days; one with nervous reactions in traffic is a source of constant worry.

CONFORMATION AND BALANCE
A good mouth, a good ride, good conformation and good balance are important points to look for. You want, if possible, to choose a pony with a well set-on head and neck; they tend to have better mouths because they can carry themselves properly, and this makes it easier when you come to school it. A good sloping shoulder and free at the elbow means a better moving pony, and you want plenty of front and a well-formed wither. There is nothing more uncomfortable than a short-fronted pony with a round wither; you feel that you are going up the neck all the time and the saddle tends to slip forward. A good front is more important than good hind-quarters.

Balance is very important in whatever pony you buy. But how do you know if it has good balance? First make sure that the withers are higher than the quarters; the other way round is a bad beginning although, of course, young ponies go through periods of growth when they are lower in front. A really well balanced pony will not lean on your hands, but will carry himself easily with good, even rhythm at all paces and will go in circles on either leg at the canter with very little effort. And a pony that goes easily into a canter and keeps cantering in circles without pulling the rider about is a pleasure to ride.

SIZE AND TYPES
Size and type depend very much on what you want the pony for. If you aspire to competition work it is best to stick to the height required by your particular age group at shows. However, this is not always possible if *one* pony has to serve several members of a family or if you happen to be very tall for your age. But whatever you do, don't choose a pony that is too large or too green for your capabilities. This just becomes a worry and is no fun at all to ride.

The *type* you choose again depends on what you want to use it for. For general hacking you want a good sturdy type, while for more competitive work a more active type with a little more quality is needed. Among the British native breeds the Welsh, New Forest, Highland, Connemara, Fells, Dales and Arabs offer a good choice. And if it is jumping that interests you the present-day winning ponies have various breeding in them. The Connemaras are outstanding for their excellent, patient temperaments and good jumping ability. They can also be very successfully crossed to a T.B. or, say, larger Welsh. The larger Welsh types, Riding Sec B's and the Cobs, either pure or crossed, are a pleasure to ride. The New Forest ponies have their own following and cross well too. The Fells and the Dales are heavier breeds and a slower type. The pure Arabs tend to be a little highly strung, but Arab blood is world famous and is found to some extent in most cross-bred ponies.

When, finally, you have found the pony of your choice and are about to conclude the purchase it is always advisable to have a veterinary certificate declaring the pony to be in sound health. Once you have paid and taken delivery of an animal you really have no possibility of taking the previous owner to task if the pony is found to be ailing. So for satisfaction on both sides seek the vet's assurance.

The height of a pony is measured in 'hands', taken from the withers to ground level.

The type of pony you choose will depend on what you want to use it for. For general hacking choose a sturdy type (perhaps a Welsh Mountain pony). For more competitive work you will need a more active type (a Connemara, for example, would be a better choice if you want to concentrate on competitive jumping). But whatever your plan, put willingness and good temperament high on your list of desirable qualities.

Shetland pony

Exmoor pony

Iceland pony

Gotland pony

Appaloosa